THE WAY

The First Christian Handbook

William Varner

University Press of America,® Inc.
Lanham · Boulder · New York · Toronto · Plymouth, UK

Copyright © 2007 by
University Press of America,® Inc.
4501 Forbes Boulevard
Suite 200
Lanham, Maryland 20706
UPA Acquisitions Department (301) 459-3366

Estover Road
Plymouth PL6 7PY
United Kingdom

Library of Congress Control Number: 2006941021
ISBN-13: 978-0-7618-3714-5 (paperback : alk. paper)
ISBN-10: 0-7618-3714-0 (paperback : alk. paper)

Dedication

I wish to dedicate this book to the students in my Intermediate Greek classes at The Master's College. Over the last decade they have worked through the language of the *Didache* with me and raised challenging questions about its translation and meaning. It was during that classroom experience that I first became convinced that I should write this book. It is my prayer that they will continue to "tremble at the words" of the one who teaches God's word to them (*Didache* 3:8-4:1).

Table of Contents

Foreword

Protestants, especially evangelicals, have not been particularly conversant with the Apostolic Fathers. And for someone who has never studied any of these ancient documents, the foray into this rich but complex world of nascent Christianity may seem daunting indeed. So many of the tomes on the Apostolic Fathers are either in a foreign language or are written for a scholarly readership that they are largely inaccessible to the interested neophyte. The initial hurdle that a beginner must get over often seems insurmountable; thus the Fathers and especially literature on them remain unread, to the spiritual and literary impoverishment of the one who has begun with noble intentions.

Enter Will Varner's *The Way of the Didache*. From the opening paragraph to the last chapter, this book engages the reader with a lively style that is borne of Varner's genuine passion for the *Didache*. I was in Jerusalem when Will got the invitation to see the lone copy of the *Didache* extant today. He and I spent lengthy conversations about this precious little book, which was rediscovered in 1873. His exuberance for the *Didache* was contagious, and it clearly comes across in this volume. Although it might be too much to say that reading Varner's tome is like reading an adventure novel, such a description seems to be only a slight exaggeration. In the least, what he has written makes the *Didache* accessible to anyone with even a passing interest in the Apostolic Fathers. But more can be said.

Varner's treatment is user friendly, written for the non-specialist. The pitch is non-combative, and the focus is on the key issues. Varner does not get bogged down in details, yet covers the major concerns related to the *Didache* comprehensively. Although his justification for this book, after so much has already been written on the *Didache*, specifies three reasons, there is also a fourth: there is a desperate need for an inviting introduction to the *Didache* that is palatable for even the motivated layperson. I can only hope that Varner's book might become a template for other volumes on other Apostolic Fathers that are written in the same manner.

Varner discusses the rediscovery of the *Didache*, noting the need for new images of this pamphlet to rectify the shortcomings in J. Rendel Harris's photographs done in 1887. With this assessment, I heartily agree. High-resolution digital photographs of the entire codex, *Hierosolymitanus* 54, are now called for to make this document fully accessible to scholars.

He argues for the unity of the book, as well as a first-century date. And not just a first-century date, but written while much of the New Testament was yet to be penned. He calls the *Didache* "the first Christian Handbook," seeing it as an instructional guide to Gentile converts. Varner also supplies the Greek text and his own translation, complete with cross-references to biblical texts. A most fascinating chapter discusses the use of Scripture in the *Didache*. In particular, I found his interaction with Andre Tuilier's argument that the Didachist used Q, calling it "The Gospel of the Lord" (and Tuilier's identification of Q as the Aramaic sayings source written by Matthew prior to the writing of his Gospel) most intriguing. In a single stroke, this suggestion both argues for an early date of the *Didache* (earlier than the canonical Matthew) and for an ancient affirmation of the existence of Q.

The sources for the *Didache*'s "Two Ways" doctrine, its primitive ecclesiology, as well as its theological motifs are also controversial topics—all of which Varner handles with an irenic tone. Some may well take issue with him over his belief that the *Didache* both has a strong theological undergirding and is a mid-first-century document. But there is much food for thought here. Varner succeeds in raising questions on numerous fronts, piquing the interest of the reader in the process.

His final chapter is eminently practical. It is almost a homily on the *Didache*, showing its relevance and importance for Christians today. Without becoming so enamored of this little tract that he loses a canonical perspective, Varner soberly exclaims, "While the *Didache* is neither the last word nor the best word on these subjects, it is a word that should be heard again—after too long a silence!" And as an evangelical, Varner in this chapter slings many an arrow into the proud heart of evangelicals whose mantra of *sola scriptura* has come to mean *nuda scriptura*. As a fellow evangelical, I applaud Will Varner for reminding us that the Teaching has something to teach us today.

Daniel B. Wallace
Executive Director
Center for the Study of New Testament Manuscripts

Preface

Because I explain the nature of this book in chapter one, I would like to express my appreciation in this preface to those who have helped in its writing. The Riddle Family Foundation and The Masters College Academic Advancement Committee provided grants that made it possible to study at Wheaton College and Tyndale House, Cambridge during a sabbatical in 2004. The librarians at all three of those institutions helped me secure materials and provided study areas for my research. Greg Beale of Wheaton Graduate School invited me to present a paper to the students there that helped to focus my research on chapter five of this book. My research assistant, Cliff Kvidahl, cheerfully conducted dozens of research projects for me. He still hopes that he will convince me some day that the *Didache* was influenced by the knowledge of the Pauline writings. My students, Melody Talcott, Dany Brodzinski and Philip Viguier translated some important French and German texts. My son, Jonathan, and former student, Kristine Briggs, proofread various parts of the book along the way. As he has done for a number of years, Abner Chou has been a great help in securing books for me, preparing the topical index, and improving my writing style by his careful proofreading of the manuscript. My faculty colleague, John Eickemeyer, and my student, Laney Stroup, helped with the intricacies of Word formatting. Daniel B. Wallace of Dallas Theological Seminary read the manuscript, made excellent suggestions, contributed the foreword, and joined me in a visit to the Greek Patriarchate Library in Jerusalem. We still have hope that he will be able someday to photograph the precious manuscript containing the *Didache* through his Center for the Study of New Testament Manuscripts.

My wife, Helen, has been an encouragement in often giving up time while I was "behind that computer." She has graciously hosted hundreds of my students on those Tuesday evenings in our home when the "Greek Geeks" gather with their professor. She also contributed to the writing of this book in ways too numerous to mention.

William Varner, Ed.D.
Santa Clarita, CA
October 27, 2006

Chapter One

Introduction to the *Didache*

The telephone call came after we had just finished our evening meal at the Knight's Palace Hotel in the Old City of Jerusalem in May 2005. The message instructed me to come now to the library of the Greek Orthodox Patriarch if I wanted to see the manuscript. I had been planning that evening to lead a group of students from The Masters College and Seminary on a walk to Ben Yehuda Street in the "new" city of Jerusalem. I excused myself, changed my clothes quickly, and began to scurry through the labyrinthine lanes of the Old City. After entering the Greek Orthodox monastery, I made my way upstairs to the library. Soon the gentle librarian, Bishop Aristarchos, delivered to me what I had waited years to see - a 950 year-old, 200-page parchment manuscript containing over a dozen individual writings from the early church. My particular interest was in a little work in the midst of the manuscript, consisting of only 10 pages (5 leaves) in length. Its name is the *Didache* (the "Teaching," pronounced "didakhay"), short for *The Teaching of the Twelve Apostles*. For the next two hours, sometimes with trembling hands, I pored over this precious document, finding answers to some questions that I had for years. Why was I so excited to see first hand this piece of parchment, the only complete manuscript copy of this work that is known to exist? And why has that experience led now to a book on the *Didache*?

Although for years I had heard of the *Didache* and understood basically what it said, I began a serious consideration of it in the Spring of 1997 when I translated sections of it with my Intermediate Greek class. In subsequent years, the class began to translate the entire document, only about the length of Paul's *Epistle to the Galatians*. I became progressively captivated by its contents and began to read and research widely in an academic area that I soon learned was quite extensive. During my sabbatical in the Spring of 2004, I made the *Didache* one of the main interests of my research in the Buswell Library of the Wheaton College and at the Tyndale House Library in Cambridge, England. By the time I attended a conference on "The New Testament and the Apostolic Fathers" at Oxford University in April, 2004, I was convinced that I should someday make my own contribution to the field of *Didache* research. The last two and a half years I have continued to lead my classes through the study of this little document, testing my ideas on them. I have personally spent hundreds of hours closely examining its contents and attempting to pull out of its chapters its "message." I have also studied intensively the scholarly issues that have been discussed by writers on this document from the 1880's until the current day. I have even made some modest contributions to the discussion—a journal article on the *Didache*'s use of scripture and a popular article on what the little book can possibly teach us about how we should "do church" today.[1] This book is the result of my now decade long love affair with the *Didache*.

In the course of studying hundreds of articles and books about the *Didache*, I have encountered many general comments about its value and the fascination it holds for its readers—far beyond what might be expected for a document its size. One of those authors opened her own article on the *Didache* with the following effusive words.

> The discovery of the *Didache* in 1873 has been acclaimed in many a eulogy, in many a language and by many a scholar. And rightly so. For this work has cast a spell over even the most cautious who, finding its magic irresistible, seek time and again to prise its secrets. For however else can one explain the unending fascination expressed in such an abundance of words for a work written with so few words—a bibliography which exceeds any reasonable expectation?[2]

If Professor Walker was amazed at the size of the bibliography on the *Didache* in 1981, what amazement would she express a quarter century later at the continued scholarly interest in this little document of less than 2,200 words? In the last decade alone, two major commentaries have been published on the *Didache*, the most recent being 800 pages in length.[3] Furthermore, within the past decade four major volumes consisting of scholarly articles on the *Didache* by multiple authors have been issued.[4] The journal articles also continue to appear at a regular pace.[5] In April, 2004, an international conference convened at Oxford University to discuss "The New Testament and the Apostolic Fathers." No less than five of the twenty five papers presented dealt directly with the *Didache* and a number of the other papers discussed indirectly issues raised by the document.[6]

The author of this book confesses to being among those people that Walker describes over whom the spell of the "Teaching" has been cast. As I translated it with my Intermediate Greek classes over the years, I was captured by its profundity in simplicity and its obvious characteristic of *multum in parvo*. As has been mentioned, this then led to its being one of the major foci of my sabbatical research, which led in turn, to the previously mentioned articles, and now, to this book. And yet, many Christians by and large neglect the study of the *Didache* particularly and the Apostolic Fathers generally. This is especially true in the case of Evangelicals (among whom I count myself), who usually leave such discussions to those who labor in the more liturgical traditions of the Church. In that regard some may be surprised that even Jewish scholars have contributed their unique perspective to this area of study.[7] It is this author's contention that the Evangelical commitment to *sola scriptura* plus their general lack of engagement with Church tradition have both contributed to their non-participation in such discussions. Therefore, only when discussions of patristic or apocryphal writings directly impact issues raised in the canonical books do Evangelicals get involved in this area of research. But the *Didache* and other early Church writings constantly discuss many issues related to New and Old Testament studies. Ought we not at least listen to and interact with what the earliest Christians wrote about these matters?

It is important to acknowledge that there is a host of other important issues that swirl around the study of the *Didache* that we hope to address in the following chapters. Some of those questions are as follows. 1. When was it discovered and what has been its history in the tradition of the Church? 2. Who was its author and when was it written? 3. What is the theological framework of the *Didache*? 4. What implications for liturgy, sacraments and ministry does it have since it appears to many to be a "church manual" in its literary genre? 5. What is its eschatological teaching, since the last chapter has often been viewed as an apocalypse? 6. What is its teaching on the Christian life and spirituality? 7. How do the things that are actually taught in the *Didache* compare to the teaching of the New Testament on these matters? These and other related issues will be explored in later chapters.[8]

Perhaps a summary of my suggested conclusions about these *Didache* issues will help to at least provide the reader with a framework for how this writer approaches the document. Without elaborating the arguments at this point, I should state that I hold to a first century date for its writing, with its provenance probably being Syria. I believe that a strong case can be made for its compositional unity, while acknowledging that it may have utilized a number of Jewish sources and have been edited by its author(s) at least once, although all versions were from the first century. It is clear to everyone that the document exemplifies a Jewish-Christian frame of reference, while addressing primarily new converts from the Gentile world. While the book is intensely practical in its philosophy of the Christian life, it is orthodox in the theological framework that underlies its writing. I am also convinced that the Didachist knew and used what was later called the *Gospel of Matthew*, although that use of *Matthew* needs to be nuanced in its details. I also will argue that the basic function of the *Didache* in the early church was as a "catechetical handbook" designed for those who were joining the Christian family from among the Gentiles.

I realize that in some of these matters, I am going against the current scholarly trend in *Didache* studies. For example, many writers on the subject now espouse the position that the Didachist did not quote *Matthew*, but both *Matthew* and *Didache* drew on earlier oral traditions attributed to Jesus.[9] Later chapters will explore these questions further and provide reasons for my adopting the above positions. I will also explore such subjects as the document's theological substructure and its overall vision for the Church and its ministry. Its contribution to eschatology and to the implications of living in the "last days" will then be explored. Finally, I offer a brief analysis of the book's language, including a complete concordance of its Greek vocabulary, which I do hope will be helpful to students and scholars who wish to dig deeper into its treasures.

The Date of the *Didache*

One of the first questions I am usually asked about the *Didache* is, "When was it written?" Occasionally some scholars have proposed a **very** early date (prior to 70 AD) for the writing of the *Didache*.[10] A safer approach is to follow Lightfoot and a number of other scholars who recognize that we are reading a document that reflects the views of a group of Jewish Christians who lived and ministered in the generation following 70 C.E. The strongest arguments for a first century provenance are: 1) the primitive simplicity of the *Didache*'s teaching about the person and work of Jesus; 2) the absence of any warning about specific doctrinal aberrations; 3) the continued existence of itinerant apostles and prophets; 4) a simple pattern for the church's leadership (overseers and deacons); and 5) its silence about any persecution experienced by its readers or writer(s). All of these characteristics seem to be uncharacteristic of the church in the first decades of the second century. Further evidence for this position will be seen as we work through the themes of the book's sixteen chapters. Although there are some exceptions, the trend of current scholarship is certainly toward a first century dating. It should also be acknowledged that a date even earlier than 70 A.D. is still possible. In my opinion, the dating of the *Didache* is directly related to the relationship of the document to canonical *Matthew*.

In his highly influential volume on the history of New Testament interpretation, Bishop Stephen Neill had this to say as he reflected on the volume by Audet (footnote ten) that had recently appeared and which argued for a pre-70 AD date.

> On the basis of an immensely learned survey of all the materials, Fr. Audet comes to the conclusion that the *Didache* was written in Syria between AD 50 and 70. It is hardly likely that this conclusion will meet with general acceptance; but it is exciting to consider the possibility that we have here a work outside the New Testament which may have been written earlier than most of the New Testament books.[11]

Hopefully, it is with that same spirit of excitement and anticipation that we approach this study of the *Didache* and its value for the Church today.

We will begin our study in the next chapter with a review of the events surrounding the modern discovery of the *Didache* and also look back on how the document was utilized in the early church. In light of the use that was made of the *Didache* in the first three centuries of its existence, I will propose my own origination hypothesis of why the book was written and how it was used. For my proposal, I will draw upon the hermeneutical method that traces the "effective history" of a text. In other words, I will ask the question, "Does the way the church utilized the document help us to understand its original purpose?

Why another Book about the *Didache*?

Before we proceed, however, I want to answer a question that some of my readers may legitimately be asking. In light of the abundance of books and articles on this little document, why should another one appear in an already crowded marketplace? The question is a fair one. An enormous amount of literature has been produced on the *Didache* in the last one hundred and twenty years. One thing that will become clear is that the early consensus about the document has changed to reflect the views of current scholars committed to various forms of source and redaction criticism. Many recent writers are very concerned to isolate the various layers of the document.[12] My work is not intended to demean the contributions of these scholars. I am concerned, however, that in the midst of all of this literary critical labor, the overall thrust of the *Didache* sometimes becomes blunted. My path will follow more in the footsteps of the earliest writers on the *Didache*, particularly those who wrote in the decade following its discovery. I believe that the modern reader will be surprised to discover that almost every issue being raised by contemporary scholars was discussed, often in detail, by these early writers. Anyone who seriously considers this little document today should be exposed to the thinking of these great scholars of the nineteenth century.[13]

Furthermore, in the scholarly writing about the *Didache* in the last decades I have found little expressed concern about the implications that this little treasure may have for the articulation of theology and the praxis of ministry in the church today. Personally, I have found that most laymen are very interested in my research into the meaning of the *Didache*. Their interest, however, is not about the arcane issues of what sources were used by the author(s) and the number of its redactors that dominate the current discussion. For those who still care about the church and its ministry, historical scholarship ought to have as at least one of its goals to conclude what, if any, are the implications that such research has for the life of the church. I realize only too well how such an idea will probably be met in some realms of academia. I am willing to face that response for the sake of my attempt at applied research. While I trust that I have not allowed such concern to prejudice my own research, the reader should know that I have always had in mind the pragmatic ministry value of the *Didache* for the church today. In this regard, I have two readers in mind. One group consists of those who want an up to date answer to the question, "What are they saying about the *Didache*?" The second group consists of those who want to know more about what a group of very early Jewish Christians had to say about doing ministry among real people in their day. Perhaps many of my readers will combine those two desires. Whether have I have succeeded in wedding those two audiences is left for the reader to decide.

Thus, the justification for another book on the *Didache* is threefold. First, it offers an approach to the *Didache* that is an alternative to much of what is written today by means of going back to the ideas of early writers on the book. Second, I draw out some practical "lessons" that can be gleaned from this pearl initially formed in the early days of Christianity, but hidden from view for a thousand years before it was again brought to the surface for our study and benefit. Third, I believe that I do offer in the book some fresh ideas about the *Didache* based on a re-examination of its fragments. Some of these fragments have survived the centuries by their embedded in the patristic writers, while others are literal fragments that survived in the sands of Egypt.

Chapter Two

The Rediscovery of the *Didache*

When I was privileged to personally examine the only known complete
Greek manuscript of the *Didache* in 2005, I experienced a real sense of euphoria
as I perused its millennium-old parchment leaves. According to the librarian's
"sign in" sheet, I was only the fourth scholar to see the manuscript in recent
years, at least in the simple record that he maintains.[14] Yet, what I felt was
probably small compared to the excitement that Philotheos Bryennios must have
had when he discovered the work buried in a larger manuscript in 1873. The
strange aspect, however, of his discovery was that he did not recognize for years
that among the other works he had found was a copy of the lost *Didache* as well!
The general account is well known and is documented in his subsequent volume,
based on the manuscript.[15] It has been re-told many times in dozens of works on
the *Didache*. Sometimes, however, we are left wondering if we know all the
details of this momentous discovery, as is the case with the romantic "story" told
by the Taamireh Bedouin about their accidental "discovery" of the seven initial
manuscripts that came to be called the "Dead Sea Scrolls."[16]

Perhaps it is best to allow Bryennios himself to relate his own story of his
discovery. In an article published soon after the publication of Bryennios' volume, an American scholar teaching in Constantinople named Edwin Grosvenor
reported in the *Andover Review* an interview that he had with the then Metro-
politan of Nicomedia. Strangely, I have not found any modern scholar that refers
to this interview. I quote it in its entirety along with its original unique punctua-
tion and other eccentric characteristics.

AN INTERVIEW WITH BISHOP BRYENNIOS –
THE DISCOVERY OF THE "TEACHING"

Last Thursday Bishop Philotheos or (as he is more commonly known in
America by his non-episcopal and family name) Bishop Bryennios, gave me a

detailed account of his discovery of the Διδαχη or Teaching manuscript, and of his subsequent connection with it. Since anything that has to do with that manuscript or with its learned discoverer is of interest, I am inclined to write down what he said, and give the reader the benefit of his remarks. As nearly as possible I shall quote his own words:

"In 1873," said the bishop, "I had been looking over the manuscripts in the Jerusalem Monastery of the Holy Sepulchre at Phanar. I had looked over them many times before, but on this occasion my eye chanced to fall on a small, thick, black volume which had always escaped my notice. Though I was about to go from the library, I said to myself, 'I will give just one glance at that book.' I found first in it the Synopsis of St. Chrysostom, which did not interest me very much. As I listlessly turned over the pages, I came next upon an epistle of Barnabas. 'What have I here?' I cried to myself; 'is it a treasure I have found? 'I carried the book with me to my house, and at once began to study it further. I thought I could not take my eyes away from the Epistle of Barnabas long enough to look at the other contents; but nevertheless I did. Directly after the Epistle of Barnabas came the first and second Epistles of Clement to the Corinthians, perhaps more precious still. 'Marvelous book! I cried. 'I will edit the Epistles of Clement and the Epistle of Barnabas, and give them to the world.' But I read on in the manuscript. A short catalogue of the holy books came next, and then immediately after, a little treatise occupying about ten pages, introduced by two inscriptions, one of which was, 'Teaching of the Twelve Apostles,' and the other 'Teaching of the Lord through the Twelve Apostles to the Nations.' The title made no impression upon my mind, I read those ten pages over; neither did they make any impression, and I passed on to the other contents of the manuscript. But one thing stood out distinctly before me. Wherever I was, whatever I was doing, I seemed to see, to think, to feel nothing but the Epistle of Barnabas and the two Epistles of Clement. Which should I study and edit first? I could not work on them both at once. I was then Bishop of Serres. I was in feeble health. The labors in my diocese occupied almost every moment of my time. At last I went back to Serres, and studied and worked and wrote every moment that I could upon the Epistles of Clement. I thought hungrily of the Epistle of Barnabas: but my comfort was in feeling that as soon as my present occupation was finished I should devote myself to that. Two years I toiled at my work, and at last it was complete; edited as carefully and as faithfully as it was in my power to do. But the Epistle of Barnabas was not yet. For several years I was sick and could only wearily drag myself about. I was promoted to the diocese of Nicomedia, and larger and more responsible cares were overtaxing my feeble strength. In seven years' time, from 1873 to 1880, I barely gave the 'Teaching' a thought. When I did think of that manuscript volume, it was only to recall the Epistles of Clement which I had edited, and to look forward to like work upon the Epistle of Barnabas. During the five years after the publication of my notes on Clement, I was in constant receipt of letters from Germany and from England, urging me to go on with the work which I had promised to do. In a foot-note I had promised, with the help of God, as soon as I was able, to give to mankind not only Barnabas, but the twelve Epistles of Ignatius, likewise contained in the volume, All these letters from Harnack, from Lightfoot, from Funk (I think also from Hilgenfeld) were upbraiding me for my delay and inciting me to fulfill my promise.

"In 1880 I again chanced to read over the Διδαχη. Something seemed to strike me like lightning. It appeared to me very different from what it did when I saw it before. Surely I had read this once, but then it did not seem the same thing as it did to me now. I was all of a tremble. This! this! this! this!' "I wish I could give the rising emphasis, the gesture, the fire in Bryennios' eye as he dwelt on the moment of realization of what he had found. " 'This must be the Διδαχη, the book that so many ancient fathers quote, the book that was lost, that the church mourns over to this day, the foundation of part of the Apostolic Constitutions. Εὕρηκα εὕρηκα εὕρηκα!' I shouted like Archimedes. From that hour I began to pore over the Teaching. Every spare moment was in some way devoted to it, until it appeared from the press in 1883. Then the letters began to flow in again faster and more numerous than they did after I had finished the Epistles of Clement; most of them flattering letters, and some of them full of gratitude at what I had done. One man who has a great name over Europe wrote, 'Hail, thou equal of the church fathers!'

"But the translations of some scholars have been so badly made and their comments so erroneous that I have gone to work again on the Teaching, and am preparing a new volume to refute and correct them. If one wants to understand it and get the spirit of it, he must feel like a Greek. Only in that degree in which one does feel like a Greek can he breathe the soul of the Teaching. And now," said the bishop, with a smile half humorous, half sad, " now that they are making me work again on this book concerning which I thought that my labors were all done, when shall I ever get to the Epistle of Barnabas? Barnabas must wait!"

Edwin A. Grosvenor.

ROBERT COLLEGE, CONSTANTINOPLE, *Sept.* 10, 1884.[17]

The spontaneity evident in the above interview along with its personal emotional touches certainly convey to the modern reader something of the sheer excitement that animated Bryennios and others who learned of his "discovery." The interview also informs us of some other important matters. Bryennios reveals that originally he intended to publish both an edition of the Two Epistles of *Clement* and the one of *Barnabas* which were in the precious manuscript that he had discovered. His important edition of the Clements did appear in 1875.[18] It was a welcome publication because the only previously known Greek manuscript of those works was that of Codex Alexandrinus, where they appear at the end of the manuscript, after the *Apocalypse*.[19] Bryennios expresses frustration that his plan to publish *Barnabas* had been delayed. He never was able to publish his own edition of *Barnabas*, although the readings of this manuscript are referenced in subsequent editions of *Barnabas* and the Apostolic Fathers. Bryennios also expresses his frustration over the "poor" translations and interpretations of the *Didache* that had appeared in the last year since his publication of the work in 1883. He wanted to publish a second edition of the book to correct these errors. Alas, there is no record of any subsequent books by Bryennios before his death in 1914. Perhaps the ill health to which he referred in the interview made it impossible for him to fulfill his further literary goals. One last comment about the discovery is also in order.

Many writers (too many to mention) have noted the fact at least two scholars in the early part of the nineteenth century catalogued the contents of the monastery library and missed the presence of the *Didache*. My own handling of the manuscript in 2005 and the recognition that it composes only five leaves in the midst of two hundred leaves has helped me to understand how that might possibly happen. The tone of naiveté displayed by Bryennios, however, makes us wish that we knew even more details about his early experience with the manuscript. We also wonder how Bryennios, by his own admission, read through the *Didache* initially without it making any "impression" on him. What did he think it was? He says only that he did not recognize it until after he published the Clement letters. And why did it hit him later like an Archimedean revelation that it was the long-lost *Didache*? Such speculation is the stuff that feeds popular conspiracy theories and novels. Since we only have Bryennios' word for it, we had best be content with his explanation and leave it at that.

In 1887 the manuscript was transferred to the Greek Orthodox Patriarch Monastery Library in Jerusalem, where it remains until today. It is catalogued as Κωδ. Παρτ. 54 and is usually referred to as "The Jerusalem Manuscript" or "H" (Hierosolymitanus 54). The manuscript consists of two hundred forty "pages" on one hundred twenty "leaves" (or folios) containing a careful minuscule script on both sides of each folio "leaf" (the *recto* and *verso*). The writing is careful but also utilizes many of the tachygraphic signs prevalent in the manuscript styles of the eleventh century. The scribe's own colophon informs us that he was named Leon (Λέων), adding, in good monastic humility, that he was a "scribe and sinner." He also provides the date when he finished copying the manuscript: the Greek dating is equivalent to Tuesday, June 11, 1056 A.D.

Leon's careful transcription of the ancient texts included not only the *Didache*, but also a number of other previously known writings attributed to various patristic authors or to people who knew them. Those works, in the order in which they are found in the Jerusalem manuscript, are as follows:

1. Synopsis of the Old and New Testaments attributed to Chrysostom: folio $1^{ro} - 38^{vo}$;
2. Epistle of Barnabas: folio $39^{ro}-51^{vo}$;
3. First Epistle of Clement: folio $51^{vo}-70^{ro}$;
4. Second Epistle of Clement: folio $70^{ro}-76^{ro}$;
5. A list of the "names of books used by the Hebrews." The titles of the books are transliterated from Hebrew into Greek with the Greek equivalents written in red ink: folio 76ro.
6. *Didache*: folio $76^{ro}-80^{vo}$;
7. A Letter by Maria of Cassoboloi to Ignatius of Antioch: folio $81^{ro}-82^{ro}$;
8. Twelve letters by Ignatius of Antioch in the secondary, longer version: folio $82^{ro}-120^{ro}$;
9. The colophon is followed by a treatise on the genealogy of Jesus: folio $120^{ro}-120^{vo}$.

The first line title in each work is also written in red ink, including that of the *Didache*: Διδαχὴ τῶν δώδεκα ἀποστόλων. J. Rendel Harris rendered the scholarly world a great service in 1887 when he published an exact transcription of the Jerusalem manuscript along with a photographic reproduction of the pages where the *Didache* is located.[20] Unfortunately the black and white photographs do not indicate the red color of the ink in the title. Furthermore, Harris cut the photograph of the first and last folio at the place where *Didache* begins and ends. This obscures the fact that the *Didache* and each work in the manuscript begins on the next line after the previous work ends (*lectio continua*). Also, one cannot clearly discern that at the end of the *Didache* Leon left six additional blank lines, each with the scribal "scoring" for the straight line, but with no text hanging from those lines! The significance of Leon's scribal activity is that he is indicating to the reader that he knows that this is not the original ending of the *Didache*, but that he is reproducing what he sees in his exemplar. More will be said later about the speculation by scholars on what the original ending of chapter 16 may have been.

The History of the *Didache*

Bryennios finally realized that the five leaves of his precious find contained an ancient book that was known to the early church but of which no manuscript had survived. What can be known about the book in the first millennium of church history? While some of the references may be legitimately contested, the evidence of the footprints left by the *Didache* is as follows.

Soon after its publication, scholars recognized that the first five chapters of the *Didache* were strikingly similar to three chapters in the well known writing generally known as the Epistle of Barnabas. The earliest scholarly view was that this section of the *Didache* showed dependence on Barnabas. This led Bryennios, therefore, to conclude that the *Didache* should be dated from 120-160 A.D.[21] He was joined in this opinion by the influential work of Adolf Harnack.[22] Other early scholars either saw the dependence in the other direction or that neither was dependent on the other but that they both went back to a common source.[23] Because of uncertainty about the relationship between the two works, it is best not to confidently assert that *Barnabas* is the first patristic document to refer to the *Didache*—although that is the view of this writer.

Clement of Alexandria is usually mentioned as the first father to cite the *Didache*, although he does not do it by name. He rather refers to a statement of "scripture" (γραφη) that calls one a thief: "Son, become not a liar, for lying leads to theft." This agrees almost word for word with *Didache* 3.5, with only a few changes of synonymous words. However, because Clement does not mention his "scripture" source by name, there have been some who are not positive about his specifically citing the *Didache*.[24] It should also be noted that in *Quis dives salvus* 29 Clement uses the phrase "Vine of David" which does not occur in any earlier work except in *Didache* 9:2.

Origen, the pupil of Clement, although again citing his source only as "divine scripture," in *De Princpiis* III.2.7, quotes *Didache* 3:10: "You will accept the experiences that happen to you as good things, knowing that nothing happens apart from God." Origen in Homily VI on the *Book of Judges* likewise used the designation of Jesus as the "Vine of David." It can legitimately be debated whether or not these two early third century "citations" are undoubtedly from the *Didache*.

From the fourth century, however, there are at least three clear references to the Didache. The first is from the church historian, Eusebius of Caesarea (d. 340). In *Ecclesiastical History*, Book III, 25 as he is discussing the books that are acknowledged as scripture, he classifies among the ecclesiastical yet uncanonical and "spurious" (νόθοις) books "The so-called Teachings of the Apostles." He uses the plural and omits the number twelve. The description "so-called," (καλούμενα) which appears also later in Athanasius, qualifies the book's apostolic origin as being only indirect, even as we speak of the "Apostles' Creed." In this same category he places *The Shepherd of Hermas* and the *Epistle of Barnabas*. These books were read in some churches, but were not important enough to be classified among the undoubted "Homologoumena" nor even among the seven "Antilegoumena" which eventually came to be recognized as part of the New Testament canon.

The second clear reference from the fourth century is from the famous *Festal Letter* of Athanasius (367). In defining what books are canonical (κα̂ νονίζομενα), he mentions the *"So-called Teaching(s) of the Apostles"* along with the *Wisdom of Solomon*, the *Wisdom of Sirach*, *Esther*, *Judith*, *Tobit*, and the *Shepherd of Hermas*. Although these books were not canonical, they were "appointed by the fathers to be read by those who are now coming to us and desiring to be instructed in the doctrine of godliness." This catechetical function of the *Didache* described by Athanasius describes how the book came to be used in the churches, certainly by the fourth century when there was a great influx into the church of converts from paganism.

The third clear reference to the *Didache* in the fourth century comes to us as a result of the discovery in 1945 of a cache of Coptic papyrus codices found in Thoura, Egypt. Most of these works are commentaries on various Biblical books written by the great head of the Catechetical School of Alexandria, Didymus the Blind. In his commentary on *Psalms* (227:26), Didymus is commenting on the verse, "Because they are speaking peaceably to me" (Ps. 34:20). He further references *Matthew* 5:9 and then elaborates on the word "peacemaker." "For this is what is said in the catechetical book of the *Didache*, 'bring peace to those who quarrel" (εν τη Διδαχη τη βιβλιω της κατηχησεως, 'ειρηνευσεις μαχομενους.'). This is a clear reference to *Didache* 4:3. In another commentary on *Ecclesiastes*, he quotes the same verse and refers to the source as "the Teaching of the Apostolic Cathechesis" (εν τη Διδαχη της κατηχεσεως). In both these references the *Didache* is tied into an apostolic provenance.

Bart Ehrman thinks that these references indicate that the NT canon of Didymus includes *Didache*.[25] However, these references and others in his commentaries that treat the *Shepherd of Hermas* as a catechetical book are consistent with the role that his patron Athanasius had assigned to these books—profitable for catechetical instruction of new converts, at least in Alexandria.

These are the clearest patristic references to the *Didache* through the fourth century. The last reference to the little book by someone who had personal knowledge of it is from the ninth century by the Patriarch of Constantinople, Nicephorus (died 828). In his *Stichometry*, he refers to a book named the *Teaching of the Apostles* (Διδαχη αποστολων) as among the New Testament apocrypha and that is consists of two hundred lines (στιχοι). From Bryennios on, many authors have noted that in the Jerusalem manuscript the *Didache* consists of two hundred and three lines. This, however, may not be as obvious as it may appear. When we compare the size of the *Didache* in the *Stichometry* with some of the other works that are mentioned, some serious questions are raised. For example, Nicephorus mentions that the combined length of the two Epistles of Clement as 2,000 lines, while in the Jerusalem manuscript they comprise 1,120 lines. Also, the length of *Barnabas* is given as 1,360 lines, which would make the *Didache's* length as about 14% that of *Barnabas*. In actuality, *Didache* is about 34% its length! Obviously, the length of Nicephorus' "stichos" is not the same as that of the Jerusalem manuscript's "line" of text. But there is another fact worth noting. If we remove chapters 7-16 of the *Didache*, the length of chapters 1-6 then is about 14% of the length of *Barnabas*. My conclusion is that whatever was the length of Nicephorus' stichos, the length of the *Didache* which he measures is not that of the book that has come down to us. I suggest that by the ninth century, the latter liturgical section of *Didache* 7-16 had become separated from the more ethical earlier section of *Didache* 1-6 and comprised the work that is referred to in Nicephorus' *Stichometry*.

In the fourth century the *Apostolic Constitutions* incorporated most of the *Didache* into its seventh chapter. Furthermore, the book's liturgical sections seemed a bit out of date with the emergence of a multileveled church hierarchy and a more ornate liturgical practice than what is described in ch. 7-15. By the ninth century the book had been evidently stripped down to its earlier ethical section. Some further confirmation of this is found in the Latin *Doctrina Apostolorum*, whose existence came to light in the late nineteenth century. It consists of only the earlier chapters of the *Didache*. A growing number of modern scholars now believe that this Latin version most closely represents the original "two ways' document that is the common source of *Didache* 1-6 and *Barnabas* 18-20.[26] While this is possible, it should also be considered that this Medieval Latin document could have been an adaptive translation of this abbreviated *Didache* that is referred to in the *Stichometry*.

We also have ancient translations of the *Didache*, such as the Coptic and Georgian versions. These are taken into consideration in the critical texts, although none of them really represents a radical departure from the Greek text of the Jerusalem manuscript. One more "remnant" of the *Didache* exists from ancient times. It is a tiny leaf from what was a miniature papyrus codex, dated to the fourth century and found among the Oxyrhynchus papyri at the end of the nineteenth century and published in 1922.[27] The leaf is written on both recto and verso in rather large letters for its size (only five by six centimeters). One side has the words of 1:3c-4a and the other has 2:7b-3:2a.[28] I believe that this tiny fragment may help us to discern how the *Didache* came to be used in Egypt in the fourth century. This miniature codex is actually the smallest example of this type of codex that has ever been found.[29] It could have easily fit into one's hand! In other words, it was probably part of a literal "handbook." The Greeks referred to such a miniature codex as an *enchiridion* (ἐγχειρίδιον).[30] The word "manual" reflects the same Latinized root.

An Origination Hypothesis

Markus Bockmuehl has written about how the "effective history" of an interpretation can help us to ascertain the originally intended meaning of the passage interpreted.[31] This is similar to tracing the history of how the passage has been understood in the history of the church. "Effective history" can serve as a guide in helping interpreters to recognize if their interpretation has also made sense to interpreters who were in the Biblical writer's future and who are a part of the modern interpreter's past. What was the "effect" that the passage had in church history? While no method is an infallible guide (what is?), the effective history of the interpretation of a non-canonical text like *Didache* can also be helpful in our arriving at an "origination hypothesis" for the original *Didache*. In other words, can the effect that the *Didache* had on the fathers who used it up until the fourth century be helpful in understanding what its original function was intended to be?

Many writers have noticed that the command to baptize in 7:1 indicates that the baptism was to take place "after you have said all these things beforehand." In other words "all these things" must refer to the instruction that had already been given in the first six chapters. It seems evident, therefore, that the first six chapters are a compendium of pre-baptismal catechetical instruction that was to be taught to recent converts from paganism to prepare them for that decisive act by which they entered the Christian community. If that was indeed the effect that the text had on later generations, it will help to confirm our explanation of why the book originated. Our brief survey of the references to the *Didache*, by such writers as Eusebius in Caesarea and Athanasius and Didymus the Blind in Egypt in the fourth century seem to confirm such an origination hypothesis.

Therefore, in light of the patristic references to the *Didache* combined with the evidence of the miniature papyrus codex, I propose that this little book was literally placed in the hands of young converts as the first "manual" of guidance for their new life. Thus I believe that we can safely conclude that the *Didache* was the first Christian Handbook of which we have written knowledge.

Chapter Three

The Text of the *Didache*

It has been noted that the text of the *Didache* is preserved in one manuscript that was discovered by Bryennios in 1873 and subsequently published in 1883. The manuscript was signed by its scribe, "Leon," and dated by him to 1056 AD. It is presently in the library of the Greek Orthodox Patriarchate in Jerusalem. The manuscript, numbered 54 in the collection, is most often referred to in text-critical terminology as "H," standing for *Hierosolymitanus*. Leon's copy has formed the basis for all subsequent study of this ancient work. The previously mentioned papyrus consisting of a small papyrus leaf containing 1.3c-4a and 2.7b-3.2a does exhibit some differences in word choice.[32] These are not sufficient, however, to dethrone the Jerusalem manuscript from its primary role in establishing the text of the document. Later versions of the *Didache* in Coptic, Georgian, and Latin serve to mainly confirm the Jerusalem text with only slight differences. Large sections of the *Didache* also appear in later documents such as the *Apostolic Constitutions* and the *Ethiopic Church Order*. Due to their secondary character, their readings that differ from H are useful only when found in combination with other identical variant readings. Thus, the Bryennios manuscript still must be the basis for a critical text.

The manuscript, however, is not perfect. Bryennios suggested a total of seventeen changes in places where he thought that Leon had clearly made an error in transcription.[33] A number of critical texts have either reproduced Bryennios' *editio princeps*[34] or have considered all the different readings suggested by various writers and produced a "conservative" eclectic text.[35] Some have taken greater liberty in omitting large sections of H or by adding passages from the later versions.[36] I have followed as the base text for my translation and study the critical text published by Rordorf and Tuilier.[37] The R/T text adopted nine of the seventeen suggested emendations by Bryennios and is careful in adopting other readings and conjectures, usually following the text critical canon of *lectio difficilior potior* (more difficult reading be preferred), and has found increasing use by scholars. I have indicated in the notes where I prefer a different reading than Rordorf and Tuilier.

ΔΙΔΑΧΗ ΤΩΝ ΔΩΔΕΚΑ ΑΠΟΣΤΟΛΩΝ

Διδαχὴ κυρίου διὰ τῶν δώδεκα ἀποστόλων τοῖς ἔθνεσιν.

1.1 Ὁδοὶ δύο εἰσί, μία τῆς ζωῆς καὶ μία τοῦ θανάτου, διαφορὰ δὲ πολλὴ μεταξὺ τῶν δύο ὁδῶν.

1.2 Ἡ μὲν οὖν ὁδὸς τῆς ζωῆς ἐστιν αὕτη· Πρῶτον ἀγαπήσεις τὸν θεὸν τὸν ποιήσαντά σε, δεύτερον τὸν πλησίον σου ὡς σεαυτόν, πάντα δὲ ὅσα ἐὰν θελήσῃς μὴ γίνεσθαί σοι, καὶ σὺ ἄλλῳ μὴ ποίει.

1.3 Τούτων δὲ τῶν λόγων ἡ διδαχή ἐστιν αὕτη· Εὐλογεῖτε τοὺς κὰ ταρωμένους ὑμῖν καὶ προσεύχεσθε ὑπὲρ τῶν ἐχθρῶν ὑμῶν, νηστεύετε δὲ ὑπὲρ τῶν διωκόντων ὑμᾶς· ποία γὰρ χάρις ἐὰν ἀγαπᾶτε τοὺς ἀ γαπῶντας ὑμᾶς; οὐχὶ καὶ τὰ ἔθνη τὸ αὐτὸ ποιοῦσιν; ὑμεῖς δὲ ἀγαπᾶτε τοὺς μισοῦντας ὑμᾶς καὶ οὐχ ἕξετε ἐχθρόν.

1.4 Ἀπέχου τῶν σαρκικῶν καὶ σωματικῶν ἐπιθυμιῶν· ἐὰν τίς σοι δῷ ῥάπισμα εἰς τὴν δεξιὰν σιαγόνα, στρέψον αὐτῷ καὶ τὴν ἄλλην καὶ ἔσῃ τέλειος· ἐὰν ἀγγαρεύσῃ σέ τις μίλιον ἕν, ὕπαγε μετ' αὐτοῦ δύο· ἐὰν ἄρῃ τις τὸ ἱμάτιόν σου, δὸς αὐτῷ καὶ τὸν χιτῶνα· ἐὰν λάβῃ τις ἀπὸ σοῦ τὸ σόν, μὴ ἀπαίτει· οὐδὲ γὰρ δύνασαι.

1.5 Παντὶ τῷ αἰτοῦντί σε δίδου καὶ μὴ ἀπαίτει· πᾶσι γὰρ θέλει δίδοσθαι ὁ πατὴρ ἐκ τῶν ἰδίων χαρισμάτων. Μακάριος ὁ διδοὺς κατὰ τὴν ἐντολήν· ἀθῶος γάρ ἐστιν. Οὐαὶ τῷ λαμβάνοντι· εἰ μὲν γὰρ χρείαν ἔχων λαμβάνει τις, ἀθῶος ἔσται· ὁ δὲ μὴ χρείαν ἔχων δώσει δίκην, ἱνατί ἔλαβε καὶ εἰς τί· ἐν συνοχῇ δὲ γενόμενος ἐξετασθήσεται περὶ ὧν ἔπραξε καὶ οὐκ ἐξελεύσεται ἐκεῖθεν, μέχρις οὗ ἀποδῷ τὸν ἔσχατον κὸ δράντην.

1.6 Ἀλλὰ καὶ περὶ τούτου δὲ εἴρηται· Ἱδρωσάτω ἡ ἐλεημοσύνη σου εἰς τὰς χεῖράς σου, μέχρις ἂν γνῷς τίνι δῷς.

2.1 Δευτέρα δὲ ἐντολὴ τῆς διδαχῆς·

2.2 Οὐ φονεύσεις, οὐ μοιχεύσεις, οὐ παιδοφθορήσεις, οὐ πορνεύσεις, οὐ κλέψεις, οὐ μαγεύσεις, οὐ φαρμακεύσεις, οὐ φονεύσεις τέκνον ἐν φθορᾷ οὐδὲ γεννηθὲν ἀποκτενεῖς, οὐκ ἐπιθυμήσεις τὰ τοῦ πλησίον.

2.3 Οὐκ ἐπιορκήσεις, οὐ ψευδομαρτυρήσεις, οὐ κακολογήσεις, οὐ μνησῖ κακήσεις.

2.4 Οὐκ ἔσῃ διγνώμων οὐδὲ δίγλωσσος· παγὶς γὰρ θανάτου ἡ διγλωσ σία.

2.5 Οὐκ ἔσται ὁ λόγος σου ψευδής, οὐ κενός, ἀλλὰ μεμεστωμένος πράξει.

2.6 Οὐκ ἔσῃ πλεονέκτης οὐδὲ ἅρπαξ οὐδὲ ὑποκριτὴς οὐδὲ κακοήθης οὐδὲ ὑπερήφανος· οὐ λήψῃ βουλὴν πονηρὰν κατὰ τοῦ πλησίον σου.

2.7 Οὐ μισήσεις πάντα ἄνθρωπον, ἀλλὰ οὓς μὲν ἐλέγξεις, περὶ ὧν δὲ προσεύξῃ, οὓς δὲ ἀγαπήσεις ὑπὲρ τὴν ψυχὴν σου.

3.1 Τέκνον μου, φεῦγε ἀπὸ παντὸς πονηροῦ καὶ ἀπὸ παντὸς ὁμοίου αὐ τοῦ.

3.2 Μὴ γίνου ὀργίλος· ὁδηγεῖ γὰρ ἡ ὀργὴ πρὸς τὸν φόνον· μηδὲ ζηλωτὴς μηδὲ ἐριστικὸς μηδὲ θυμικός· ἐκ γὰρ τούτων ἁπάντων φόνοι γεννῶνται.

3.3 Τέκνον μου, μὴ γίνου ἐπιθυμητής, ὁδηγεῖ γὰρ ἡ ἐπιθυμία πρὸς τὴν πορνείαν, μηδὲ αἰσχρολόγος μηδὲ ὑψηλόφθαλμος· ἐκ γὰρ τούτων ἁπάντων μοιχεῖαι γεννῶνται.

3.4 Τέκνον μου, μὴ γίνου οἰωνοσκόπος, ἐπειδὴ ὁδηγεῖ εἰς τὴν εἰδωλό λατρίαν, μηδὲ ἐπαοιδὸς μηδὲ μαθηματικὸς μηδὲ περικαθαίρων, μηδὲ θέλε αὐτὰ βλέπειν < μηδὲ ἀκούειν >[38] ἐκ γὰρ τούτων ἁπάντων εἰδωλολατρία γεννᾶται.

3.5 Τέκνον μου, μὴ γίνου ψεύστης, ἐπειδὴ ὁδηγεῖ τὸ ψεῦσμα εἰς τὴν κλοπήν, μηδὲ φιλάργυρος μηδὲ κενόδοξος· ἐκ γὰρ τούτων ἁπάντων κλο παὶ γεννῶνται.

3.6 Τέκνον μου, μὴ γίνου γόγγυσος, ἐπειδὴ ὁδηγεῖ εἰς τὴν βλασφημίαν, μηδὲ αὐθάδης μηδὲ πονηρόφρων· ἐκ γὰρ τούτων ἁπάντων βλασφημίαι γεννῶνται.

3.7 Ἴσθι δὲ πραΰς· ἐπεὶ οἱ πραεῖς κληρονομήσουσι τὴν γῆν.

3.8 Γίνου μακρόθυμος καὶ ἐλεήμων καὶ ἄκακος καὶ ἡσύχιος καὶ ἀγαθὸς καὶ τρέμων τοὺς λόγους διὰ παντός, οὓς ἤκουσας.

3.9 Οὐχ ὑψώσεις σεαυτὸν οὐδὲ δώσεις τῇ ψυχῇ σου θράσος. Οὐ κολληθήσεται ἡ ψυχή σου μετὰ ὑψηλῶν, ἀλλὰ μετὰ δικαίων καὶ τὰ πεινῶν ἀναστραφήσῃ.

3.10 Τὰ συμβαίνοντά σοι ἐνεργήματα ὡς ἀγαθὰ προσδέξῃ, εἰδὼς ὅτι ἄτερ Θεοῦ οὐδὲν γίνεται.

4.1 Τέκνον μου, τοῦ λαλοῦντός σοι τὸν λόγον τοῦ Θεοῦ μνησθήσῃ νυκτὸς καὶ ἡμέρας, τιμήσεις δέ αὐτὸν ὡς Κύριον· ὅθεν γὰρ ἡ κυριότης λαλεῖται, ἐκεῖ κύριός ἐστιν.

4.2 Ἐκζητήσεις δὲ καθ' ἡμέραν τὰ πρόσωπα τῶν ἁγίων, ἵνα ἐπαναπαῇς τοῖς λόγοις αὐτῶν.

4.3 Οὐ ποιήσεις σχίσμα, εἰρηνεύσεις δὲ μαχομένους· κρινεῖς δικαίως, οὐ λήψῃ πρόσωπον ἐλέγξαι ἐπὶ παραπτώμασιν.

4.4 Οὐ διψυχήσεις, πότερον ἔσται ἢ οὔ.

4.5 Μὴ γίνου πρὸς μὲν τὸ λαβεῖν ἐκτείνων τὰς χεῖρας, πρὸς δὲ τὸ δοῦναι συσπῶν.

4.6 Ἐὰν ἔχῃς διὰ τῶν χειρῶν σου, δώσεις λύτρωσιν ἁμαρτιῶν σου.

4.7 Οὐ διστάσεις δοῦναι οὐδὲ διδοὺς γογγύσεις· γνώσῃ γὰρ τίς ἐστιν ὁ τοῦ μισθοῦ καλὸς ἀνταποδότης.

4.8 Οὐκ ἀποστραφήσῃ τὸν ἐνδεόμενον, συγκοινωνήσεις δὲ πάντα τῷ ἀδελφῷ σου καὶ οὐκ ἐρεῖς ἴδια εἶναι· εἰ γὰρ ἐν τῷ ἀθανάτῳ κοινωνοί ἐστε, πόσῳ μᾶλλον ἐν τοῖς θνητοῖς;

4.9 Οὐκ ἀρεῖς τὴν χεῖρά σου ἀπὸ τοῦ υἱοῦ σου ἢ ἀπὸ τῆς θυγατρός σου, ἀλλὰ ἀπὸ νεότητος διδάξεις τὸν φόβον τοῦ Θεοῦ.

4.10 Οὐκ ἐπιτάξεις δούλῳ σου ἢ παιδίσκῃ, τοῖς ἐπὶ τὸν αὐτὸν Θεὸν ἐλπίζουσιν, ἐν πικρίᾳ σου, μήποτε οὐ μὴ φοβηθήσονται τὸν ἐπ' ἀμφοτέροις Θεόν· οὐ γὰρ ἔρχεται κατὰ πρόσωπον καλέσαι, ἀλλ' ἐφ' οὓς τὸ πνεῦμα ἡτοίμασεν.

4.11 Ὑμεῖς δὲ οἱ δοῦλοι ὑποταγήσεσθε τοῖς κυρίοις ὑμῶν ὡς τύπῳ Θεοῦ ἐν αἰσχύνῃ καὶ φόβῳ.

4.12 Μισήσεις πᾶσαν ὑπόκρισιν καὶ πᾶν ὃ μὴ ἀρεστὸν τῷ κυρίῳ.

4.13 Οὐ μὴ ἐγκαταλίπῃς ἐντολὰς κυρίου, φυλάξεις δὲ ἃ παρέλαβες, μήτε προστιθεὶς μήτε ἀφαιρῶν.

4.14 Ἐν ἐκκλεσίᾳ ἐξομολογήσῃ τὰ παραπτώματά σου καὶ οὐ προσελεύσῃ ἐπὶ προσευχήν σου ἐν συνειδήσει πονηρᾷ. Αὕτη ἐστὶν ἡ ὁδὸς τῆς ζωῆς.

5.1 Ἡ δὲ τοῦ θανάτου ὁδός ἐστιν αὕτη· Πρῶτον πάντων πονηρά ἐστι καὶ κατάρας μεστή· φόνοι, μοιχεῖαι, ἐπιθυμίαι, πορνεῖαι, κλοπαί, εἰδῶ λολατρίαι, μαγεῖαι, φαρμακίαι, ἁρπαγαί, ψευδομαρτυρίαι, ὑποκρίσεις, διπλοκαρδία, δόλος, ὑπερηφανία, κακία, αὐθάδεια, πλεονεξία, αἰσχρολό γία, ζηλοτυπία, θρασύτης, ὕψος, ἀλαζονεία,·ἀφοβία·[39]

5.2 διῶκται ἀγαθῶν, μισοῦντες ἀλήθειαν, ἀγαπῶντες ψεῦδος, οὐ γινώσκοντες μισθὸν δικαιοσύνης, οὐ κολλώμενοι ἀγαθῷ οὐδὲ κρίσει δικαίᾳ, ἀγρυπνοῦντες οὐκ εἰς τὸ ἀγαθόν, ἀλλ᾽ εἰς τὸ πονηρόν· ὧν μά κρὰν πραΰτης καὶ ὑπομονή, μάταια ἀγαπῶντες, διώκοντες ἀνταπόδομα, οὐκ ἐλεοῦντες πτωχόν, οὐ πονοῦντες ἐπὶ καταπονουμένῳ, οὐ γινώσκοντες τὸν ποιήσαντα αὐτούς, φονεῖς τέκνων, φθορεῖς πλάσματος Θεοῦ, ἀποστρεφόμενοι τὸν ἐνδεόμενον, καταπονοῦντες τὸν θλιβόμενον, πλουσίων παράκλητοι, πενήτων ἄνομοι κριταί, πανθαμάρτητοι, ῥυσθείητε, τέκνα, ἀπὸ τούτων ἁπάντων.

6.1 Ὅρα, μή τίς σε πλανήσῃ ἀπὸ ταύτης τῆς ὁδοῦ τῆς διδαχῆς, ἐπεὶ παρεκτὸς Θεοῦ σε διδάσκει.

6.2 Εἰ μὲν γὰρ δύνασαι βαστάσαι ὅλον τὸν ζυγὸν τοῦ κυρίου, τέλειος ἔσῃ· εἰ δ᾽ οὐ δύνασαι, ὃ δύνῃ τοῦτο ποίει.

6.3 Περὶ δὲ τῆς βρώσεως, ὃ δύνασαι βάστασον· ἀπὸ δὲ τοῦ εἰδωλοθύτου λίαν πρόσεχε· λατρεία γάρ ἐστιν Θεῶν νεκρῶν.

7.1 Περὶ δὲ τοῦ βαπτίσματος οὕτω βαπτίσατε: ταῦτα πάντα προεῖ πόντες βαπτίσατε εἰς τὸ ὄνομα τοῦ πατρὸς καὶ τοῦ υἱοῦ καὶ τοῦ ἁγίου πνεύματος ἐν ὕδατι ζῶντι.

7.2 Ἐὰν δὲ μὴ ἔχῃς ὕδωρ ζῶν, εἰς ἄλλο ὕδωρ βάπτισον· εἰ δ᾽ οὐ δύνασαι ἐν ψυχρῷ, ἐν θερμῷ.

7.3 Ἐὰν δὲ ἀμφότερα μὴ ἔχῃς, ἔκχεον εἰς τὴν κεφαλὴν τρὶς ὕδωρ εἰς ὄνομα πατρὸς καὶ υἱοῦ καὶ ἁγίου πνεύματος.

7.4 Πρὸ δὲ τοῦ βαπτίσματος προνηστευσάτω ὁ βαπτίζων καὶ ὁ βαπτι ζόμενος καὶ εἴ τινες ἄλλοι δύνανται· κελεύεις δὲ νηστεῦσαι τὸν βαπτι ζόμενον πρὸ μιᾶς ἢ δύο.

8.1 Αἱ δὲ νηστεῖαι ὑμῶν μὴ ἔστωσαν μετὰ τῶν ὑποκριτῶν· νηστεύσουσι γὰρ δευτέρᾳ σαββάτων καὶ πέμπτῃ· ὑμεῖς δὲ νηστεύσατε τετράδα καὶ παρασκευήν.

8.2 Μηδὲ προσεύχεσθε ὡς οἱ ὑποκριταί, ἀλλ' ὡς ἐκέλευσεν ὁ κύριος ἐν τῷ εὐαγγελίῳ αὐτοῦ, οὕτως προσεύχεσθε·

Πάτηρ ἡμῶν ὁ ἐν τῷ οὐρανῷ,
Ἁγιασθήτω τὸ ὄνομά σου,

Ἐλθέτω ἡ βασιλεία σου,
Γενηθήτω τὸ θέλημά σου ὡς ἐν οὐρανῷ καὶ ἐπὶ γῆς·
Τὸν ἄρτον ἡμῶν τὸν ἐπιούσιον δὸς ἡμῖν σήμερον,
Καὶ ἄφες ἡμῖν τὴν ὀφειλὴν ἡμῶν,
Ὡς καὶ ἡμεῖς ἀφίεμεν τοῖς ὀφειλέταις ἡμῶν,
Καὶ μὴ εἰσενέγκῃς ἡμᾶς εἰς πειρασμόν,

Ἀλλὰ ῥῦσαι ἡμᾶς ἀπὸ τοῦ πονηροῦ·

Ὅτι σοῦ ἐστὶν ἡ δύναμις καὶ ἡ δόξα εἰς τοὺς αἰῶνας.

8.3 Τρὶς τῆς ἡμέρας οὕτω προσεύχεσθε.

9:1 Περὶ δὲ τῆς εὐχαριστίας, οὕτως εὐχαριστήσατε·

9.2 πρῶτον περὶ τοῦ ποτηρίου·

Εὐχαριστοῦμέν σοι πάτερ ἡμῶν,
Ὑπὲρ τῆς ἁγίας ἀμπέλου Δαυεὶδ τοῦ παιδός σού
Ἧς ἐγνώρισας ἡμῖν διὰ Ἰησοῦ τοῦ παιδός σου·
Σοὶ ἡ δόξα εἰς τοὺς αἰῶνας.

9.3 Περὶ δὲ τοῦ κλάσματος·

Εὐχαριστοῦμέν σοι πάτερ ἡμῶν,
Ὑπὲρ τῆς ζωῆς καὶ γνώσεως,
Ης ἐγνώρισας ἡμῖν διὰ Ἰησοῦ τοῦ παιδός σου·

Σοὶ ἡ δόξα εἰς τοὺς αἰῶνας.

9.4   Ὥσπερ ἦν τοῦτο τὸ κλάσμα διεσκορπισμένον ἐπάνω
       τῶν ὀρέων καὶ συναχθὲν ἐγένετο ἕν,
       Οὕτω συναχθήτω σου ἡ ἐκκλησία ἀπὸ τῶν περάτων
       τῆς γῆς εἰς τὴν σὴν βασιλείαν·

       Οτι σοῦ ἐστιν ἡ δόξα καὶ ἡ δύναμις διὰ Ἰησοῦ Χριστοῦ εἰς
       τοὺς αἰῶνας.

9.5 Μηδεὶς δὲ φαγέτω μηδὲ πιέτω ἀπὸ τῆς εὐχαριστίας ὑμῶν, ἀλλ' οἱ
βαπτισθέντες εἰς ὄνομα κυρίου· καὶ γὰρ περὶ τούτου εἴρηκεν ὁ κύριος·
((Μὴ δῶτε τὸ ἅγιον τοῖς κυσί.))

10:1 Μετὰ δὲ τὸ ἐμπλησθῆναι οὕτως εὐχαριστήσατε·

10.2   Εὐχαριστοῦμέν σοι, πάτερ ἅγιε,
       Ὑπὲρ τοῦ ἁγίου ὀνόματός σου,
       Οὗ κατεσκήνωσας ἐν ταῖς καρδίαις ἡμῶν,
       Καὶ ὑπὲρ τῆς γνώσεως καὶ πίστεως καὶ ἀθανασίας,
       Ἧς ἐγνώρισας ἡμῖν διὰ Ἰησοῦ τοῦ παιδός σου·
       Σοὶ ἡ δόξα εἰς τοὺς αἰῶνας.

10.3   Σύ, δέσποτα παντοκράτορ,
       Ἔκτισας τὰ πάντα ἕνεκεν τοῦ ὀνόματός σου,
       Τροφήν τε καὶ ποτὸν ἔδωκας τοῖς ἀνθρώποις εἰς ἀπόλαυσιν, ἵνα
       σοι εὐχαριστήσωσιν.
       Ἡμῖν δὲ ἐχαρίσω πνευματικὴν τροφὴν καὶ ποτὸν καὶ ζωὴν
       αἰώνιον διὰ⁴⁰ τοῦ παιδός σου.

10.4   Πρὸ πάντων εὐχαριστοῦμέν σοι ὅτι δυνατὸς εἶ·
       Σοὶ ἡ δόξα εἰς τοὺς αἰῶνας.

10.5   Μνήσθητι, κύριε, τῆς ἐκκλησίας σου τοῦ ῥύσασθαι αὐτὴν ἀπὸ
       παντὸς πονηροῦ,

       Καὶ τελειῶσαι αὐτὴν ἐν τῇ ἀγάπῃ σου,

Καὶ σύναξον αὐτὴν ἀπὸ τῶν τεσσάρων ἀνέμων, τὴν ἁγιασθεῖσαν,
Εἰς τὴν σὴν βασιλείαν ἣν ἡτοίμασας αὐτῇ·

Ὅτι σοῦ ἐστιν ἡ δύναμις καὶ ἡ δόξα εἰς τοὺς αἰῶνας.

10.6 Ἐλθέτω χάρις καὶ παρελθέτω ὁ κόσμος οὗτος.

Ὡσαννὰ τῷ θεῷ Δαυείδ.
εἴ τις ἅγιός ἐστιν ἐρχέσθω· εἴ τις οὐκ ἔστι μετανοείτω·

Μαρὰνάθά· ἀμήν.

10.7 Τοῖς δὲ προφήταις ἐπιτρέπετε εὐχαριστεῖν, ὅσα θέλουσιν.[41]

11:1 Ὃς ἂν οὖν ἐλθὼν διδάξῃ ὑμᾶς ταῦτα πάντα τὰ προειρημένα, δέξασθε αὐτόν·

11.2 ἐὰν δὲ αὐτὸς ὁ διδάσκων στραφεὶς διδάσκῃ ἄλλην διδαχὴν εἰς τὸ καταλῦσαι, μὴ αὐτοῦ ἀκούσητε· εἰς δὲ τὸ προσθεῖναι δικαιοσύνην καὶ γνῶσιν κυρίου, δέξασθε αὐτὸν ὡς κύριον.

11.3 Περὶ δὲ τῶν ἀποστόλων καὶ προφητῶν κατὰ τὸ δόγμα τοῦ εὐαγγελίου οὕτω ποιήσατε.

11.4 Πᾶς δὲ ἀπόστολος ἐρχόμενος πρὸς ὑμᾶς δεχθήτω ὡς κύριος·

11.5 οὐ μενεῖ δὲ <εἰ μη>[42] ἡμέραν μίαν· ἐὰν δὲ ᾖ χρεία, καὶ τὴν ἄλλην· τρεῖς δὲ ἐὰν μείνῃ, ψευδοπροφήτης ἐστίν.

11.6 Ἐξερχόμενος δὲ ὁ ἀπόστολος μηδὲν λαμβανέτω εἰ μὴ ἄρτον, ἕως οὗ αὐλισθῇ· ἐὰν δὲ ἀργύριον αἰτῇ, ψευδοπροφήτης ἐστί.

11.7 Καὶ πάντα προφήτην λαλοῦντα ἐν πνεύματι οὐ πειράσετε οὐδὲ διακρινεῖτε· πᾶσα γὰρ ἁμαρτία ἀφεθήσεται αὕτη δὲ ἡ ἁμαρτία οὐκ ἀφεθήσεται.

11.8 Οὐ πᾶς δὲ ὁ λαλῶν ἐν πνεύματι προφήτης ἐστίν, ἀλλ' ἐὰν ἔχῃ τοὺς τρόπους κυρίου. Ἀπὸ οὖν τῶν τρόπων γνωσθήσεται ὁ ψευδοπροφήτης καὶ ὁ προφήτης.

11.9 Καὶ πᾶς προφήτης ὁρίζων τράπεζαν ἐν πνεύματι, οὐ φάγεται ἀπ᾽ αὐτῆς, εἰ δὲ μήγε, ψευδοπροφήτης ἐστί.

11.10 Πᾶς δὲ προφήτης διδάσκων τὴν ἀλήθειαν, εἰ ἃ διδάσκει οὐ ποιεῖ, ψευδοπροφήτης ἐστί.

11.11 Πᾶς δὲ προφήτης δεδοκιμασμένος, ἀληθινός, ποιῶν εἰς μυστήριον κοσμικὸν ἐκκλησίας, μὴ διδάσκων δὲ ποιεῖν, ὅσα αὐτὸς ποιεῖ, οὐ κριθήσεται ἐφ᾽ ὑμῶν· μετὰ θεοῦ γὰρ ἔχει τὴν κρίσιν· ὡσαύτως γὰρ ἐποίησαν καὶ οἱ ἀρχαῖοι προφῆται.

11.12 Ὃς δ᾽ ἂν εἴπῃ ἐν πνεύματι· δός μοι ἀργύρια ἢ ἕτερά τινα, οὐκ ἀκούσεσθε αὐτοῦ· ἐὰν δὲ περὶ ἄλλων ὑστερούντων εἴπῃ δοῦναι, μηδεὶς αὐτὸν κρινέτω.

12:1 Πᾶς δὲ ὁ ἐρχόμενος ἐν ὀνόματι κυρίου δεχθήτω· ἔπειτα δὲ δοκὶ μάσαντες αὐτὸν γνώσεσθε, σύνεσιν γὰρ ἕξετε δεξιὰν καὶ ἀριστεράν.

12.2 Εἰ μὲν παρόδιός ἐστιν ὁ ἐρχόμενος, βοηθεῖτε αὐτῷ, ὅσον δύνασθε· οὐ μενεῖ δὲ πρὸς ὑμᾶς εἰ μὴ δύο ἢ τρεῖς ἡμέρας, ἐὰν ᾖ ἀνάγκη.

12.3 Εἰ δὲ θέλει πρὸς ὑμᾶς καθῆσθαι, τεχνίτης ὤν, ἐργαζέσθω καὶ φαγέτω.

12.4 Εἰ δὲ οὐκ ἔχει τέχνην, κατὰ τὴν σύνεσιν ὑμῶν προνοήσατε, πῶς μὴ ἀργὸς μεθ᾽ ὑμῶν ζήσεται χριστιανός.

12.5 Εἰ δ᾽ οὐ θέλει οὕτω ποιεῖν, χριστέμπορός ἐστι· προσέχετε ἀπὸ τῶν τοιούτων.

13:1 Πᾶς δὲ προφήτης ἀληθινὸς, θέλων καθῆσθαι πρὸς ὑμᾶς, ἄξιός ἐστι τῆς τροφῆς αὐτοῦ.

13.2 Ὡσαύτως διδάσκαλος ἀληθινός ἐστιν ἄξιος καὶ αὐτὸς ὥσπερ ὁ ἐρ γάτης τῆς τροφῆς αὐτοῦ.

13.3 Πᾶσαν οὖν ἀπαρχὴν γενημάτων ληνοῦ καὶ ἅλωνος, βοῶν τε καὶ προβάτων λαβὼν δώσεις τὴν ἀπαρχὴν τοις προφήταις· αὐτοὶ γάρ εἰσιν οἱ ἀρχιερεῖς ὑμῶν.

13.4 Ἐὰν δὲ μὴ ἔχητε προφήτην, δότε τοῖς πτωχοῖς.

13.5 Ἐὰν σιτίαν ποιῇς, τὴν ἀπαρχὴν λαβὼν δὸς κατὰ τὴν ἐντολήν.

13.6 Ὡσαύτως κεράμιον οἴνου ἢ ἐλαίου ἀνοίξας, τὴν ἀπαρχὴν λαβὼν δὸς τοῖς προφήταις·

13.7 ἀργυρίου δὲ καὶ ἱματισμοῦ καὶ παντὸς κτήματος λαβὼν τὴν ἀ παρχήν ὡς ἄν σοι δόξῃ, δὸς κατὰ τὴν ἐντολήν.

14:1 Κατὰ κυριακὴν δὲ κυρίου συναχθέντες κλάσατε ἄρτον καὶ εὐχᾶ ριστήσατε, προσεξομολογησάμενοι τὰ παραπτώματα ὑμῶν, ὅπως καθαρὰ ἡ θυσία ὑμῶν ᾖ.

14.2 Πᾶς δὲ ἔχων τὴν ἀμφιβολίαν μετὰ τοῦ ἑταίρου αὐτοῦ μὴ σύ νελθέτω ὑμῖν, ἕως οὗ διαλλαγῶσιν, ἵνα μὴ κοινωθῇ ἡ θυσία ὑμῶν.

14.3 Αὕτη γὰρ ἐστιν ἡ ῥηθεῖσα ὑπὸ κυρίου· ((Ἐν παντὶ τόπῳ καὶ χρόνῳ προσφέρειν μοι θυσίαν καθαράν. ὅτι βασιλεὺς μέγας εἰμί, λέγει κύριος, καὶ τὸ ὄνομά μου θαυμαστὸν ἐν τοῖς ἔθνεσι.))

15:1 Χειροτονήσατε οὖν ἑαυτοῖς ἐπισκόπους καὶ διακόνους ἀξίους τοῦ κυρίου, ἄνδρας πραεῖς καὶ ἀφιλαργύρους καὶ ἀληθεῖς καὶ δεδοκί μασμένους· ὑμῖν γὰρ λειτουργοῦσι καὶ αὐτοὶ τὴν λειτουργίαν τῶν προφητῶν καὶ διδασκάλων.

15.2 Μὴ οὖν ὑπερίδητε αὐτούς· αὐτοὶ γάρ εἰσιν οἱ τετιμημένοι ὑμῶν μετὰ τῶν προφητῶν καὶ διδασκάλων.

15.3 Ἐλέγχετε δὲ ἀλλήλους μὴ ἐν ὀργῇ, ἀλλ' ἐν εἰρήνῃ, ὡς ἔχετε ἐν τῷ εὐαγγελίῳ· καὶ παντὶ ἀστοχοῦντι κατὰ τοῦ ἑτέρου μηδεὶς λαλείτω μηδὲ παρ' ὑμῶν ἀκουέτω, ἕως οὗ μετανοήσῃ.

15.4 Τὰς δὲ εὐχὰς ὑμῶν καὶ τὰς ἐλεημοσύνας καὶ πάσας τὰς πράξεις οὕτω ποιήσατε, ὡς ἔχετε ἐν τῷ εὐαγγελίῳ τοῦ κυρίου ἡμῶν.

16:1 Γρηγορεῖτε ὑπὲρ τῆς ζωῆς ὑμῶν· οἱ λύχνοι ὑμῶν μὴ σβεσθήτωσαν, καὶ αἱ ὀσφύες ὑμῶν μὴ ἐκλυέσθωσαν, ἀλλὰ γίνεσθε ἕτοιμοι· οὐ γὰρ οἴδατε τὴν ὥραν, ἐν ᾗ ὁ κύριος ἡμῶν ἔρχεται.

16.2 Πυκνῶς δὲ συναχθήσεσθε ζητοῦντες τὰ ἀνήκοντα ταῖς ψυχαῖς ὑμῶν· οὐ γὰρ ὠφελήσει ὑμᾶς ὁ πᾶς χρόνος τῆς πίστεως ὑμῶν, ἐὰν μὴ ἐν τῷ ἐσχάτῳ καιρῷ τελειωθῆτε.

16.3 Ἐν γὰρ ταῖς ἐσχάταις ἡμέραις πληθυνθήσονται οἱ ψευδοπροφῆται καὶ οἱ φθορεῖς, καὶ στραφήσονται τὰ πρόβατα εἰς λύκους, καὶ ἡ ἀγάπη στραφήσεται εἰς μῖσος.

16.4 Αὐξανούσης γὰρ τῆς ἀνομίας μισήσουσιν ἀλλήλους καὶ διώξουσι καὶ παραδώσουσι, καὶ τότε φανήσεται ὁ κοσμοπλανὴς ὡς υἱὸς θεοῦ καὶ ποιήσει σημεῖα καὶ τέρατα, καὶ ἡ γῆ παραδοθήσεται εἰς χεῖρας αὐτοῦ, καὶ ποιήσει ἀθέμιτα, ἃ οὐδέποτε γέγονεν ἐξ αἰῶνος.

16.5 Τότε ἥξει ἡ κτίσις τῶν ἀνθρώπων εἰς τὴν πύρωσιν τῆς δοκιμᾶ σίας, καὶ σκανδαλισθήσονται πολλοὶ καὶ ἀπολοῦνται, οἱ δὲ ὑπομείναντες ἐν τῇ πίστει αὐτῶν σωθήσονται ὑπ᾽ αὐτοῦ τοῦ κᾶ ταθέματος.

16.6 Καὶ τότε φανήσεται τὰ σημεῖα τῆς ἀληθείας· πρῶτον σημεῖον ἐκ πετάσεως ἐν οὐρανῷ, εἶτα σημεῖον φωνῆς σάλπιγγος, καὶ τὸ τρίτον ἀνάστασις νεκρῶν.

16.7 οὐ πάντων δέ, ἀλλ᾽ ὡς ἐρρέθη· ((Ἥξει ὁ κύριος καὶ πάντες οἱ ἅγιοι μετ᾽ αὐτοῦ.))

16.8 Τότε ὄψεται ὁ κόσμος τὸν κύριον ἐρχόμενον ἐπάνω τῶν νεφελῶν τοῦ οὐρανοῦ . . .

Chapter Four

A Translation of the *Didache*

Brief Explanation: This is a new translation of the *Didache* that seeks to understand its thought flow through portraying visually clauses that are sequential, subordinate or parallel. I have utilized this approach in my own exegetical analysis of the Greek New Testament writings. I also gratefully acknowledge the labors of Aaron Milavec in his ground-breaking work on the *Didache*.[43] While not woodenly literal, the translation philosophy employed tends toward what some call the "formal equivalence" rather than the "functional equivalence" approach to translation. For example, whenever there is a clear μεν. . .δε contrastive construction, I have utilized the literal translation "on the one hand. . .on the other hand" to bring out the contrast implied. This may appear to be overly pedantic in some verses, but it will be helpful for a close examination of the point being made by the author(s) of the *Didache*.

As is the case in some NT epistles, the second person singular is sometimes used to address the reader and sometimes the second person plural is used. In translating the second person, the "you" and "your" forms in English do not convey whether the Greek form is singular or plural. I have found helpful the practice of Aelred Cody in his excellent translation and have adapted it for this translation.[44] In chapters 1-6, the second person *singular* form is usual in the Greek and should be understood in the English translation. The exceptional use of the plural form is indicated in these chapters by the insertion of [pl]. In chapters 7-16, the second person *plural* form is usual in the Greek and should be understood in the translation. The exceptional use of the singular form is indicated by the insertion of [sg.]. Although this may appear a bit unwieldy at times, the shifts back and forth from singularity to plurality are important for the critical study of the document.

In the translation, I have bolded what I believe to be quotations or clear citations of canonical Old and New Testament passages and have also included the passage cited in parentheses after the quotation. Possible allusions to non-

canonical books have not been bolded, but the suggested passage that may be
alluded to has also been placed in parentheses. Discussion of these possible quotations, citations, and allusions will take place in a later chapter.

Teaching of the Twelve Apostles

Teaching of the Lord through the Twelve Apostles to the Gentiles

1:1 There are two ways: one of **life** and one of **death**!
      And there is a great difference between the two ways.
      (cf. Mt 7:13,14; Dt 30:19; Pr 1-9)
1:2 [A] On the one hand, then, the way of life is this:
          [1] **first: you will love the God** who made you;
          [2] **second: your neighbor as yourself.**
          (Matt 22:37-39; Deut. 6:5; Lev 19:18)
    [B] On the other hand:
          as many things as you wish not to happen to you,
          likewise, do not do to another. (cf. Matt 7:12)

1:3 And concerning these words, the teaching is this:
      [A] **speak** [pl. rest of verse] **well of the ones speaking badly of you,**
      [B] **and pray** for your enemies,
      [C] and fast **for the ones persecuting you;**
          For what merit is there if you love the ones who love you?
          Do not even the Gentiles do the same thing?
      [D] **on the other hand, love the ones who hate you, (Matt 5:44-47)**
      and you will not have any enemy.

1:4 Abstain from fleshly and bodily desires. (cf. I Peter 2:11)

      [A] **If anyone should strike you on the right cheek,**
          turn to him also the other, (Matt 5:39) and you will be perfect;
          (Matt 5:48)
      [B] **if anyone should press you into service for one mile,**
          go with him two;
      [C] **if anyone should take away your cloak,**
          give to him also your tunic;
      [D] **if anyone should take from you what is yours,**
          do not ask for it back; (Matt 5:41, 40)
      for you are not even able to do so.
1:5 **To everyone asking you for anything, give it**
      and do not ask for it back; (Luke 6:30/ /Matt. 5:42)
          for, to all, the Father wishes to give
          these things from his own free gifts.
      [A] Blessed is the one who gives according to the commandment;

for he is guiltless.

[B] Woe to the one who takes;

 [1] for, on the one hand, if anyone having need takes,
  he will be blameless;

 [2] On the other hand, the one not having need

  [a] will stand trial
   as to why he received and for what use;

  [b] and being in prison, he will be examined thoroughly concerning the things he has done,

  [c] **and he will not come out from there until he pays back the last cent.** (cf. Matt 5:26; Luke 12:59)

1:6 [C] But also, concerning this, on the other hand, it has been said:

 "Let your alms sweat in your hands,
 until you know to whom you should give it." (see Sirach 12:1,7)

2:1 And the second command of the teaching:

2:2 [A1] **You will not murder,**

 [A2] **you will not commit adultery,**   **(Matt 19:18; 5:33)**

 [A3] you will not corrupt children,

 [A4] you will not have illicit sex,

 [A5] you will not steal,

 [A6] you will not practice magic,

 [A7] you will not make potions,

 [A8] you will not murder a child by means of abortion,

 [A9] nor you will kill one that has been born,

 [A10] you will not desire the things of your neighbor.

2:3 [B1] you will not swear falsely, (Matt 5:33 ?)

 [B2] you will not bear false witness,

 [B3] you will not speak evil of anyone,

 [B4] you will not hold grudges.

2:4 [B5] You will not be double-minded nor double-tongued,
 for being double-tongued is a snare of death.

2:5 Your word will not be false nor empty,
  but will be fulfilled in action.

2:6 [C1] You will not be covetous,

 [C2] nor greedy,

 [C3] nor a hypocrite,

 [C4] nor spiteful,

 [C5] nor arrogant. (2:2-6 elaborate Ex. 20:13-17)

You will not plot an evil plan against your neighbor.

2:7 You will not hate any person,
  [1] but some you will reprove,
  [2] and for others you will pray,
  [3] and some you will love more than your soul.

3:1 My child, flee from every evil
    and from everything like it.

3:2 [A] Do not become angry,
        for anger leads to murder;
      nor be envious,
      nor be contentious,
      nor be hot-headed,
        for, from all these, murders are born.
3:3 [B] My child, do not become lustful,
        for lust leads to illicit sex;
      nor use foul speech,
      nor be one who lifts up the eyes,
        for, from all these, adulteries are born.

3:4 [C] My child, do not practice divination,
        since this leads to idolatry;
      nor be an enchanter,
      nor be an astrologer,
      nor be a magician,
      nor even wish to see nor hear these things,
        for, from all these, idolatry is born.
3:5 [D] My child, do not become false,
        since falsehood leads to theft;
      nor be a lover of money,
      nor be a seeker of glory,
        for, from all these, thefts are born.

3:6 [E] My child, do not become a grumbler,
        since this leads to blasphemy;
      nor be a self-pleaser,
      nor be evil-minded,
        for, from all these, blasphemies are born.

3:7 But be meek,
      since **the meek will inherit the earth. (Matt. 5:5; Ps. 37:11)**

3:8 [A] Become long-suffering
        and merciful
        and harmless

and gentle
and good
and one who trembles always at the words
　　that you have heard.　(allusion to Isaiah 66:2)

3:9 [B] You will not exalt yourself,
　　　　and you will not give boldness to your soul.
　　　　Your soul will not be joined with the haughty,
　　　　but with just and lowly people you will dwell.

3:10 [C] You will accept the experiences that happen to you as good things,
　　　　knowing that, apart from God, nothing happens.

4:1 [A] My child, the one speaking to you the word of God,
　　　　[1] you will remember night and day,　(cf. Heb 13:7)
　　　　[2] and you will honor him as the Lord,
　　　　　　for where the dominion of the Lord is spoken of,
　　　　　　there is the Lord.
4:2　　[3] And you will seek every day the presence of the saints
　　　　　　in order that you may find support in their words.

4:3 [B] You will not cause division,
　　　　[1] and you will reconcile those who quarrel;
　　　　[2] you will judge justly,
　　　　[3] you will not show favoritism
　　　　　　when you reprove others for their failings.
4:4 [C] You will not be double-minded whether it will be or not.
4:5 [A] Do not become one,
　　　　[1] on the one hand, who stretches out your hands to receive,
　　　　[2] on the other hand, draws them back from giving.

4:6 [B] If you should have something through the work of your hands,
　　　　you will give it as a ransom for your sins.
4:7　　[1] You will not hesitate to give,
　　　　[2] nor will you grumble when you give;
　　　　　　for you will know who will be
　　　　　　the good paymaster of your reward.

4:8 [C] You will not turn away the one in need;
　　　　[1] but you will share together all things with your brother
　　　　[2] and you will not say that such things **are your own**; (Acts 4:32)
　　　　　　for, if you (pl.) are partners in what is immortal,
　　　　　　how much more [are you partners] in the mortal things?

4:9 [A] You will not take away your hand

from your son or from your daughter,
but from youth you will teach them the fear of God.

4:10 [B] You will not command your male or female slave
who are hoping in the same God
in your bitterness,
lest they should never fear the God who is over you both;
for He does not come to call according to social status,
but those whom the Spirit has prepared.

4:11 [C] And you (pl.), slaves, will be subject to your masters
as to the image of God in shame and fear.

4:12 [A] You will hate all hypocrisy
and everything that is not pleasing to the Lord.

4:13 [B] Never forsake the commandments of the Lord,
but you will guard the things that you have received,
neither adding nor subtracting anything. (Deut 4:2 or 12:32)

4:14 [C] In church, you will confess your wrongdoings,
and you will not go to your place of prayer with an evil conscience.
This is the way of life!

5:1 The way of death, on the other hand, is this:

First of all, it is evil and full of accursedness:

[A1] murders,	[A12] duplicity,
[A2] adulteries,	[A13] deceit,
[A3] lusts,	[A14] arrogance,
[A4] sexual immoralities,	[A15] malice,
[A5] thefts,	[A16] stubbornness,
[A6] idolatries,	[A17] greed,
[A7] feats of magic,	[A18] foul-speech,
[A8] potions,	[A19] jealousy,
[A9] robberies,	[A20] audacity,
[A10] perjuries,	[A21] haughtiness,
[A11] hypocrisies,	[A22] boastfulness;

5:2   [B1] persecutors of the good,
[B2] hating truth,
[B3] loving a lie,
[B4] not knowing the wages of righteousness,
[B5] not cleaving to the good,
[B6] nor to just judgment,

[B7] those who are on the alert
    not for the good,
    but for the evil thing;
[B8] far from being gentle and patient,
[B9] loving empty things,
[B10] pursuing retribution,
[B11] not showing mercy to the poor,
[B12] not working for the oppressed,
[B13] not knowing the one who made them,
[B14] murderers of children,
[B15] destroyers of what God has formed,
[B16] turning away the one in need,
[B17] oppressing the afflicted,
[B18] advocates of the rich,
[B19] unjust judges of the poor,
[B20] totally sinful.

May you (pl.) be delivered, children, from all of these!

6:1 See to it that no one leads you astray from this way of teaching,
    since he is teaching you apart from God.
6:2   [1] For, on the one hand, if you are able to bear
        the whole yoke of the Lord, you will be perfect;
    [2] but if, on the other hand, you are not able,
        that which you are able, do this.

6:3 And concerning food,
    [1] bear that which you are able,
    [2] but from the food sacrificed to idols,
        especially keep away
            for it is [related to] the worship of dead gods.

7:1 And concerning baptism, baptize this way:

    After you have said all these things beforehand,
    immerse in the name of the Father
        and of the Son
        and of the Holy Spirit (Matt 28:19)
    in flowing water.

7:2 [1] but if you (sg., as in rest of verses 2-4) do not have flowing water,
        immerse in other water;
    [2] and if you are not able to do so in cold,
        [immerse] in warm [water];

7:3 [3] and if you should not have either,
pour out water onto the head three times
in the name of the Father
and of the Son
and of the Holy Spirit.

7:4 And prior to the baptism,
[1] let the one baptizing fast;
[2] also one being baptized
[3] and if any others are able to do so;
And order the one being baptized to fast
one or two [days] before.

8:1 And let your fasts
not be with the hypocrites, (cf. Matt 6:16)
for they fast on the second
and on the fifth days of the week;   (cf. Lk. 18:12)
but you should fast during the fourth day
and the preparation day. (see Mk.15:42; Jn.19:14, 31)

8:2 And do not pray like the hypocrites, (cf. Matt 6:5)
but like the Lord commanded in his gospel.

Pray this way:

Our Father, who is in heaven,
May your name be kept holy,
May your kingdom come,
May your will be done on earth as in heaven;
Give us today our daily bread,
And forgive us our debt,
As we also forgive our debtors,
And do not lead us into trial,
But deliver us from the evil one;   (Matt. 6:9-13)
Because yours is the power and the glory forever.

8:3 Three times daily pray this way. (cf. Ps. 55:17)

9:1 And concerning the thanksgiving meal, give thanks this way:

9:2 First, concerning the cup:

We give you thanks, our Father,
For the holy vine of your **servant** David
Which you revealed to us through your **servant** Jesus.
To you is the glory forever.

9:3 And concerning the broken bread:

> We give you thanks, our Father,
> For the life and knowledge,
> Which you revealed to us through your **servant** Jesus.
> To you is the glory forever. **(Isaiah 52:13)**

9:4 Just as this broken bread was scattered over the mountains,
>   and was gathered together and became one,
> In this way, may your church be gathered together
>   from the ends of the earth into your kingdom.
> Because yours is the glory and the power
>   through Jesus Christ forever.

9:5 And let no one eat or drink from your thanksgiving meal
>   except those baptized in the name of the Lord,
>   for also the Lord has said concerning this:
>   **"Do not give what is holy to the dogs."** **(Matt. 7:6)**

10:1 And after being filled, give thanks in this way:

10:2 We give you thanks, holy Father,
> For your holy name,
> Which you have caused to dwell in our hearts,
> And for the knowledge and faith and immortality
> Which you revealed to us through your **servant** Jesus.
> To you is the glory forever.

10:3 You, almighty Master,
> Created all things for the sake of your name,
> Both food and drink you have given to people for enjoyment
>   in order that they might give thanks.
> But to us you have graciously bestowed spiritual food and drink and
>   eternal life through your servant.

10:4 Before all things, we give you thanks because you are powerful.
> To you is the glory forever.

10:5 Remember, Lord, your church,
>   to save her from every evil,
>   and to perfect her in your love
>   and to **gather her together from the four winds,** **(Matt. 24:31)**
>   the sanctified into your kingdom which you prepared for her.
> Because yours is the power and the glory forever.

10:6 [A] May grace come and may this world pass away!
> [B] Hosanna to the God of David! (cf. Matt. 21:9)

[C] If anyone is holy, let him come!
If anyone is not, let him repent!
[D] **Come Lord** [maranatha]! Amen! (cf. I Cor. 16:22)

10:7   But allow the prophets to "give thanks" as much as they wish.

11:1   [A] Therefore, whoever teaches you all these things said previously,
receive him.
11:2   [B] If, on the other hand, the one teaching,
if he has been turned,
and should teach another doctrine
[1] for the destroying [of those things],
do not listen to him.
[2] But, if it is for the bringing of righteousness
and knowledge of the Lord,
receive him as the Lord!

11:3   And concerning the apostles and prophets in accord with the decree of
the gospel, act thus:

11:4[A] Every apostle coming to you, let him be received as the Lord.
11:5   [1] But he will not remain except for one day,
[2] and if there is a need, also another [day].
[3] But if ever he should remain three [days], he is a false prophet.
11:6   [B] And, when he departs,
[1] let the apostle take nothing except bread [that he needs]
until he is lodged.
[2] If, however, he asks for money, he is a false prophet.

11:7   [A] And every prophet speaking in the Spirit
you should not test nor judge,
for every sin will be forgiven,
but this sin will not be forgiven. (cf. Matt 12:31)
11:8   [B] But not everyone speaking in the Spirit is a prophet,
but only if he has the behavior of the Lord.
Therefore, from their behavior will be known the false prophet
and the prophet.

11:9   [A] And every prophet ordering a table in the Spirit,
will not eat from it, and if he does, he is a false prophet.
11:10   [B] And every prophet teaching the truth,
if he does not do what he teaches, he is a false prophet.
11:11   [C] And every prophet who has been put to the test and is genuine,
and who acts for the earthly mystery of the church,
but not teaching to do what he himself does,

he shall not be judged by you;
　　　for he has his judgment from God,
　　　for also the ancient prophets so acted.

11:12　[D] But whoever should say in the Spirit,
　　　[1] "Give me silver or any other thing,"
　　　you will not listen to him.
　　　[2] But if he should say to give to others in need,
　　　let no one judge him.

12:1 And everyone coming in the name of the Lord,
　　　let him be received;
　　　and then, having put him to the test,
　　　you will know,
　　　for you will have understanding of right and left.

12:2[A] If, on the one hand, the one coming is passing through,
　　　[1] help him as much as you are able.
　　　[2] He will not remain, however, among you
　　　　　except for two or three days,
　　　　　if there should be a need.

12:3　[B] If, on the other hand, he wishes to settle down among you,
　　　and if he is a craftsman, let him work and let him eat.

12:4　[C] If, on the other hand, he does not have a craft,
　　　according to your own understanding, plan beforehand
　　　how he will live among you as a **Christian**, without being idle.

12:5　[D] If, on the other hand, he does not wish to behave this way,
　　　he is a Christ-peddler.
　　　Beware of such ones!

13:1　[A] And every genuine prophet wishing to settle down among you
　　　is worthy of his food.

13:2　[B] Likewise a genuine teacher is **worthy,
　　　just as the laborer, of his food. (Matt. 10:10)**

13:3　[A] So, you (sg.) shall take every first fruits of the produce
　　　from the wine vat and threshing floor,
　　　of both cattle and sheep,
　　　[1] and you (sg.) will give the first fruits to the prophets,
　　　　　for they themselves are your (pl.) high-priests.

13:4　　　[2] But if you (pl.) do not have a prophet,
　　　　　give it to the poor.

13:5　[B] If you (sg., vss. 5-7) should make bread,
　　　take the first fruits,
　　　and give according to the commandment.

13:6　[C] Similarly, when you open a jar of wine or of oil,
　　　take the first fruits,

          and give it to the prophets.
13:7   [D] And of silver and of clothing and of every possession,
              take the first fruits,
                   as it seems good to you, and give according to the command-
                   ment.

14:1   And on the Lord's day of the Lord,
         when you are gathered together, break bread.
         [A] And give thanks, having before confessed your failings,
              so that your sacrifice may be pure.
14:2   [B] However, let no one having a conflict with his comrade,
              come together with you,
                   until they have been reconciled,
                        in order that your sacrifice may not be defiled.
                        (cf. Matt 5:23, 24)

14:3   For this [sacrifice] is that which was spoken by the Lord:
              "In every place and time, offer to me a pure sacrifice."
              "Because I am a great king," says the Lord,
              "and my name will be wondrous among the Gentiles."
              (Malachi 1:11,14)

15:1   [A] Appoint, then, for yourselves,
              overseers and deacons worthy of the Lord, (cf. Phil. 1:1)
              [1] gentle men
              [2] and not money lovers
              [3] and truthful
              [4] and tested;
                   for they likewise conduct among you
                   the ministry of the prophets and teachers.
15:2   [B] Do not, then, look down upon them;
                   for they themselves are your honored ones
                   along with the prophets and teachers.
15:3   [A] And correct one another, not in anger, but in peace,
              as you have it in the gospel. (see Matt 18:15-18)
         [B] And to everyone wronging another,
              [1] let no one speak to him
              [2] nor let anyone hear from you about him,
                   until he repents.
15:4   And **do your prayers and alms and all your actions**
         as you have it in the gospel of our Lord. (see **Matt. 6:1-4; 5-15**)

16:1   [A] Be watchful over your life;
              [1] do not let your lamps be quenched,

[2] and do not let your waists be ungirded. (Matt. 25:8; Luke 12:35?)

[B] But be prepared,
for you do not know the hour in which our Lord is coming. (Matt 24:42)

16:2   [C] And frequently be gathered together,
seeking what is appropriate for your souls;
for the whole time of your faith will not benefit you
unless you are perfected in the end time.

16:3   [1] For, in the last days
[a] the false prophets and corrupters will be multiplied,
[b] and the sheep will be turned into wolves,
[c] and the love will be turned into hatred.
16:4   **For, when lawlessness increases,**
[a] they will hate each other
[b] and they will persecute
[c] and they will betray each other. (Matt 24:10-12)

[2] And then will appear the world-deceiver as a son of God,
[a] and he will do signs and wonders, (Matt 24:24)
[b] and the earth will be delivered into his hands,
[c] and he will do unlawful things
that never have happened from eternity.

16:5   [3] Then the human creation will come
into the fiery test,
[a] and **many will be led into sin** and will perish,
[b] but the **ones remaining firm in their faith,**
will be saved (Matt 24:10,13) by the curse itself.

16:6   [4] And then the signs of the truth will appear: (cf. Matt 24:30)
[a] first, a sign of an opening in heaven,
[b] then a sign of a trumpet sound, (Matt 24:30; I Thess. 4:16)
[c] and the third [sign will be] a resurrection of dead ones--
16:7   but not of all [the dead],
but as it was said:
"The Lord will come and all the holy ones with him." (Zech. 14:5; cf. I Thess. 3:13)

16:8   [5] Then the world will see the Lord **coming atop the clouds of heaven . . .** (cf. Matt 24:30; 26:64; Daniel 7:13 LXX)

Chapter Five

The Scriptures of the *Didache*

One of the most important current issues in Biblical studies is that of the New Testament's use of Old Testament passages and themes with the resulting implications for inspiration and hermeneutics that such use raises.[45] A related but neglected issue is how early Christian writers outside the New Testament canon handled the authoritative sources of their own "scriptures." This issue should also be considered as we develop our own hermeneutical methodology of how interpreters today should utilize citations from scripture. Do the Apostolic Fathers cite the Old Testament in the same way as the New Testament writers? Furthermore, when they did they refer to the writings that came to be called the New Testament, how did they cite them? In this chapter we examine how the Didachist cited the Old Testament scriptures and then how he interpreted and applied them to his concerns. We will also examine the question of whether he cited any written "gospel" or oral tradition coming from Jesus. Then we will briefly address the question of whether he utilized what would today be called non-canonical writings. Each of these issues raises questions about the correct use of terminology, especially the meaning of the word "canonical."

The two main issues facing the student of this subject are: 1) In what **form** does the writer cite Scripture (e.g., the LXX or the Masoretic Text) and 2) In what **manner** does the writer use the Scriptural text to make the point? Both of these questions (the linguistic and the hermeneutical) must be squarely faced in studying the Scriptures of the *Didache*. As a working model, I propose the following paradigm that has been suggested by many writers but is cogently described by David Aune.

In *citations*, a portion of text is reproduced word for word from a source, often prefaced with an introductory formula such as "As it is written" (Rom. 9:13), "For the scripture says to Pharaoh" (Rom. 9:17), "Have you not read this scripture" (Mark 12:10-11). Distinguished from citations are *quotations*, word-for-word reproductions of a text without any introductory markers. *Allusions* are references that the writer assumes the reader will recognize . . . consisting of one or more words sufficiently distinctive to be traced to a known text, but not a verbatim reproduction of any part of that text. An *echo* is subtler than an allusion and is a relatively faint reference to a text.[46]

Certainty about authorial intent tends to diminish the more one progresses through that paradigm from *citations* to *echoes*. Whatever be the case, the paradigm remains useful not only for how the New refers to the Old but also how the Didachist and later writers refer back to the canonical books. There are examples in the *Didache* of each of these ways of referring to scripture suggested by Aune.

Use of the Old Testament
We begin this study of the *Didache*'s use of Scripture by noting its two direct citations from the OT. The first is a significant citation from Malachi 1:11, 14. The Didachist employs it at the end of a section in chapter 14 in which he exhorts the brethren to be at peace with one another lest they mar their own participation in the eucharist. He makes a point (similar to Matt. 5:23, 24) that one's eucharistic sacrifice could be defiled as long as there exists unreconciled differences between brethren. He then cites the OT text that he believes prophesies of sacrifices to be kept by the Gentiles.

14:3 For this is that which was spoken by the Lord: (ἡ ῥηθεῖσα)
    "In every place and time, offer to me a pure sacrifice."
    "Because I am a great king," says [the] Lord,
    "and my name is wondrous among the Gentiles." **(Mal. 1:11, 14)**

A comparison of the text form of the Didachist's citation reveals some differences with both the Masoretic and LXX forms of the verses (note words in bold type).

[*Didache*: Ἐν παντὶ τόπῳ καὶ χρόνῳ προσφέρειν μοι θυσίαν καθαράν.
ὅτι βασιλεὺς μέγας εἰμί λέγει κύριος
καὶ τὸ ὄνομά μου **θαυμαστὸν** ἐν τοῖς ἔθνεσι.

MT: וּבְכָל־מָקוֹם מֻקְטָר מֻגָּשׁ לִשְׁמִי וּמִנְחָה טְהוֹרָה
כִּי מֶלֶךְ גָּדוֹל אָנִי אָמַר יְהוָה צְבָאוֹת וּשְׁמִי נוֹרָא בַגּוֹיִם:

LXX: ἐν παντὶ τόπῳ θυμίαμα προσάγεται τῷ ὀνόματί μου καὶ θυσία καθαρά. διότι βασιλεὺς μέγας ἐγώ εἰμι λέγει κύριος **παντοκράτωρ** καὶ τὸ ὄνομά μου **ἐπιφανὲς** ἐν τοῖς ἔθνεσιν.]

The Didachist omits the title "Almighty" from Mal. 1:11 (צְבָאוֹת in MT; παντοκράτωρ in LXX) and utilizes a functionally equivalent word (θαυμαστὸν) for the נוֹרָא of Mal. 1:14 in the MT and the ἐπιφανὲς in the LXX.

Of greater interest is why he may have chosen Malachi 1:11, 14 and how he saw its function in redemptive history. The Didachist probably seized on the Malachi prophecy because of its reference to the Gentiles (ἔθνεσι) in verse 14. It should be kept in mind that he sees his work as the "Teaching of the Lord through the Twelve Apostles to the Gentiles." The prophecy about Gentiles offering a pure sacrifice when Malachi's Jewish people were offering defiled sacrifices (Malachi 1:6-10) implies a reversal of what the Jewish people of Malachi's day knew and observed. The Didachist saw these future sacrifices as spiritual, fulfilled in the eucharistic observances commemorating the one great sacrifice for them through Jesus. A large number of church fathers followed the Didache in viewing the Malachi prophecy as finding its fulfillment in the eucharistic observance in the assemblies of (predominantly) Gentile believers.[47] One wonders if these later writers were influenced by the Didache in this regard. NT writers do not cite the Malachi text but probably echo it when they describe believers in this new age as offering spiritual sacrifices (Hebrews 13:15, 16; I Peter 2:5; Phil. 2:17; 4:18).

The other instance of the Didache citing a specific OT text is in the last chapter of his work. Chapter 16 has often been referred to as the "little apocalypse" and will be treated more fully in a later chapter because of the hermeneutical issues it raises. We will be looking now at how the Didachist grounds his point about the bodily resurrection that will accompany the second advent in a prophecy from Zechariah 14:5.

16:6   [4] And then the signs of the truth will appear:
       [a] [the] first sign [will be] an opening in heaven,
       [b] then [the] sign of a trumpet sound,
       [c] and the third [sign will be] a resurrection of dead ones-

16:7   but not of all [the dead], (οὐ πάντων δε)
    but as it was said: (ἐρρέθη)
    "The Lord will come and all the holy ones with him."

[*Didache*: ἥξει ὁ κύριος καὶ πάντες οἱ ἅγιοι μετ' αὐτοῦ.

MT: וּבָא יְהוָה אֱלֹהַי כָּל־קְדֹשִׁים עִמָּךְ:

LXX: ἥξει κύριος ὁ θεός μου καὶ πάντες οἱ ἅγιοι μετ' αὐτοῦ]

The Didachist does not claim that his "teaching" in this chapter is some special or new revelation. This would be inconsistent with his goal to present the "teaching of the Apostles." He simply is taking material that echoes the

"Olivet Discourse" of Matt. 24, 25 plus OT parallels and adapting them to his perception of the order in which those events will transpire. The Didachist, on the basis of his understanding of eschatological passages as a whole, does not envision a general resurrection as taking place, but one that consists only of believers (οὐ πάντων δε 16:7a). He believes that this is consistent with the prophecy in Zech. 14:5 about "the holy ones" who will accompany the Lord (κύριος) when he will come (ἥξει). The only issue of textual form here is that the *Didache* quotation agrees with the LXX reading "with Him" (μετ' αὐτοῦ) instead of the reading "with you" (עִמָּךְ) of the MT. The *Didache* interprets the "holy ones" of Zech. 14:5 as referring to believers, not to angels (cf. I Thess. 2:13). Elsewhere, the NT sees angels as also accompanying the Lord at His advent (Matt. 25:30).

This is not the place to engage in an adequate exegesis of the surrounding text and its eschatological details. It should be noted, however, that some writers have seen strong chiliastic implications in the Didachist's view of a resurrection that will be limited to believers only.[48] The argument, however, is not certain because the Didache breaks off at this point and we simply do not know what followed in the original ending, which all agree is missing in the Bryennios manuscript discovered in 1873.[49]

In addition to these clear citations of two OT texts, the Didachist adapts many of the Torah commandments in Exodus into his ethical treatise in chapters 2-5. He presents his commands with a wisdom motif similar to that used in Proverbs. Consider, for example, his use of the repeated "teknon mou" phrase in 3:1, 3, 5, 6 and 4:3 with its echoes from Solomon's address to "my son" 15 times in Proverbs 1-9. In addition to the wisdom tradition of Proverbs, there is a similar approach in the non-canonical wisdom book, Jesus ben Sirach. Throughout the Greek version of that book a "teknon" is addressed no less than 19 times and then is given instruction in behavior similar to that prescribed in the Didache (Sirach 2:1; 3:12, 17; 4:1; 6:18, 23, 32; 10:28; 14:11; 16:24; 21:1; 30:9; 31:22; 37:27; 38:9, 16; 40:28). While it may be that the Didachist is not directly quoting Proverbs or Sirach, he is echoing a literary pattern that was prevalent in Jewish wisdom literature.

Use of the New Testament

The reader of the *Didache* who is familiar with the New Testament will be struck by the fact that it is hard to discern in it any clear reference to the writings of Paul, Peter and John. The same reader, on the other hand, will also be struck by its apparent fondness for the Gospel of Matthew. A good case could be made that the Didachist cites **only** that Gospel and possibly also that of Luke. The general question of how writers cite Scripture is complicated by the question of what constitutes a quotation of an earlier work. How accurate to the original source does it have to be to qualify as a "quotation"?

Before we examine some specific examples of how the Didachist may refer to Matthew, it would be helpful to see the amazing extent to which he does just that. The following table shows how often that verses very similar to Matthew appear in the *Didache*.

The *Didache* and Matthew

Didache Reference	Matthew Reference
Title	28:16, 19, 20
1:1	7:13, 14
1:2	22:38, 39
1:2e	7:12
1:3b	5:44
1:3c	5:46,47
1:4b	5:39, 48, 40, 41
1:5a	5:42, 45
1:5b	5:26
2:2	5:21; 19:18
2:3	5:33
3:2	5:21, 22
3:3	5:27, 28
3:7	5:5
3:8	5:7
5:1b	15:19
7:1	28:19
8:1	6:16
8:2a	6:2, 5, 16
8:2c	6:9-13
9:5b	7:6
11:1,2	5:17,19,20
11:7	12:31
13:1	10:10
14:2	5:24
16:1	24:42; 25:13
16:3	24:11, 12
16:4	24:10, 12
16:5	24:10
16:6	24:30, 31
16:8	24:30

There are many who would not agree that every one of these verses in *Didache* is a deliberate reference to a Matthean passage. For example, some of the references in the table from *Didache* 2:2-3:7 could possibly refer to various verses in the LXX text of Exodus and Psalm 37, although they do match Matthew's version of them in Greek. Despite possible differences about some of the verses, the sheer number of the possible parallels confirms to the casual reader that at least the shadow of the first Gospel is evident in the *Didache.*

Upon further examination of this table one notices that the vast bulk of possible quotations (25 of 31) are either from the Sermon on the Mount (Matt. 5-7) or the Olivet Discourse (Matt. 24-25)—the two longest discourses of Jesus in Matthew's gospel. Another striking thing to notice is that there is really only one other passage in *Didache* where it appears that his Gospel quotation agrees more closely with a Synoptic Gospel other than Matthew. That is in *Didache* 1:5a.[50] The following chart illustrates the relationship between the three texts.

Didache 1:5a in Matthew and Luke

Didache text of 1:5a	Luke 6:30	Matthew 5:42
παντὶ τῷ αἰτοῦντι σε δίδου καὶ μὴ ἀπαίτει·	παντὶ αἰτοῦντί σε δίδου, καὶ . . . μὴ ἀ παίτει.	τῷ αἰτοῦντί σε δός καὶ . . . μὴ ἀποστραφῇς.

Such variation between the texts prevents us from blind dogmatism about *Didache*'s sole usage of Matthew. The rarity of divergence, however, certainly illustrates the point that the Didachist used a text like that of Matthew's almost exclusively.

It is necessary at this point to address the question about whether the Didachist (or any Apostolic Father for that matter) actually knew the Gospel of Matthew or any Gospel in the canonical form that we know them. In this matter, *Didache* scholars are currently divided. Up until the 1950's writers on the *Didache* almost universally held that the Didachist knew and used our canonical Matthew.[51] The most thorough defense of the view that the *Didache* knew and used Matthew is the extensive 1950 study by Edouard Massaux.[52] With the publication of Helmut Koester's doctoral thesis under Rudolph Bultmann in 1957, the terrain of "use of Matthew" began to change.[53] The Bultmann/Koester disciples declare, among other reasons, that since our canonical Gospels did not take final shape until well into the second century, it is impossible that the *Didache* could have used them, unless it was by one of its later redactors.[54] The magisterial 1958 tome of Jean Paul Audet also effectively argued for the non-use of Matthew in the *Didache*.[55] These authors usually point to the fluidity in the evangelical tradition in these works and also how verses often do not appear in the same context in which they are found in canonical Matthew. The exact quotations that do appear, however, are usually explained as later redactions intended to bring the quotations in line with their later written form. Therefore, according to this approach, all that the Didachist and many of the Apostolic Fathers had at their disposal was the oral tradition of Jesus' words which was heavily marked by fluidity and diversity. And that diversity is often illustrated by the very citations in the Fathers' writings.

However, not all scholars have surrendered to the currently prevailing "negative" view and many still argue that it is entirely possible that the *Didache* and other early Fathers did utilize material from the Synoptic Gospels. If this usage was not always by direct quotation, then certainly it was by strong enough allusions to indicate their knowledge of the Gospels. Such writers also have provided the hard evidence to show this to be the case.[56] One recent work from a contemporary NT scholar affirms, "The *Didache* means by 'the gospel' [8:2; 11:3; 15:3, 4] the Gospel of Matthew; thus the *Didache* . . . documents the emerging authority of the one great Gospel."[57] Schnelle's references to those places in the *Didache* where τὸ εὐαγγελίον appear indicate that the writer had a written Gospel before him. Note especially the expression in 15:3 and repeated in 15:4: ὡς ἔχετε ἐν τῷ εὐαγγελίῳ τοῦ κυρίου ἡμῶν. The words that the Didachist quotes from what he calls the εὐαγγελιον are words that are found in canonical Matthew only. Martin Hengel also confidently affirms, "At some points the written character (of Matthew) emerges quite clearly, as in the *Didache*, which surely knew Matthew."[58] The usual response to this evidence from the *Didache* is to declare that these verses were added by a later redactor. Thus it may appear that only the presupposition that Matthew couldn't have existed at the end of the first century is what keeps some scholars from admitting that it could be quoted in the *Didache*. The evidence, however, points in another direction!

But just as there is great similarity with Matthew, what can be said about the differences in the details of how the Didachist cites Matthew? How do we explain those differences? An examination of *Didache* 1:3-5a, for example, certainly indicates that these verses are not transferred verbatim from Matthew's gospel. They appear to be freely adapted from Matthew 5:39-41 and 44-48. The differences, on the one hand, can be explained by recognizing that the Didachist adapted these passages for his didactic purpose, much like what some NT authors do. Also modern teachers and preachers may adapt a passage to their purpose without necessarily changing the authorial intent of the passage. This is the explanation persuasively argued in Christopher Tuckett's seminal article cited above (endnote 56) and also one that is in accordance with common sense practice. After a detailed analysis of *Didache* 1:3-5a, Tuckett concluded, "The Didachist was using his sources here with a certain degree of faithfulness. This suggests very strongly that the *Didache* here presupposes the gospels of Matthew and Luke in their finished forms. Further, this result seems to apply to all parts of the *Didache* examined here."[59]

Should we expect exactness in quotation from all ancient writers? Do we expect the same precision in the Biblical writers that meets modern scholarly standards? The Fathers wrote what they did, not to be read as academic term papers graded by pedantic teaching assistants, but for the practical purpose of instructing and exhorting their readers. This teaching proceeded from passionate hearts, sometimes even quoting from memory. Consider the words of the great textual scholar, Bruce Metzger about the quoting habits of the Fathers.

> After the true text of the Patristic author has been recovered, the further question must be raised whether the writer intended to quote the scriptural passage verbatim or merely to paraphrase it. If one is assured that the Father makes a

bona fide quotation and not a mere allusion, the problem remains whether he quoted it after consulting the passage in a manuscript or whether he relied on his memory.[60]

Metzger goes on to illustrate how Origen hardly ever quoted the same passage in the same way twice! Perhaps we should grant the Didachist the benefit of the doubt if he occasionally fashioned the Matthew verses to fit his teaching purpose. When he does change the wording slightly, he appears always to be consistent with the authorial intent of Jesus as recorded in Matthew.

Emphasizing the divergences of the *Didache* text from Matthew obscures the fact that differences are actually few compared to similarities. For most of his other citations/quotations there is no significant difference between the texts. Consider, for example, two specific examples of the Didachist's quoting of Matthew (in 8:2 and 9:5).

Intense ethical instruction composes most of chapters 1-6 of the *Didache*. The Didachist then proceeds to describe how a church should conduct its ministry of sacraments, prayer, teaching and hospitality (chapters 7-15). He does this by utilizing the discourse marker περὶ δε no less than five times; to mark off the sections in which he gives instruction on 1) dietary restrictions (6:3); 2) baptism and prayer (7:1); 3) the eucharist (9:1, 3); and 4) the treatment of apostles and prophets (11:3).[61]

In the section on prayer, he commends praying as follows.

> 8:2 "(And) do not pray like the hypocrites
>   but like the Lord commanded in his gospel.

> Pray this way:

>> Our Father, who is in heaven,
>> may your name be made holy,
>> may your kingdom come,
>> may your will be done upon earth as in heaven,
>> give us today our daily bread,
>> and forgive us our debt
>> as we also forgive our debtors,
>> and do not lead us into trial
>> but deliver us from the evil one,
>> **because yours is the power and the glory forever."**

> [*Didache*: Πάτηρ ἡμῶν ὁ ἐν τῷ **οὐρανῷ**, ἁγιασθήτω τὸ ὄνομά σου, ἐ
>   λθέτω ἡ βασιλεία σου, γενηθήτω τὸ θέλημά σου ὡς ἐν οὐ
>   'ρανῷ καὶ ἐπὶ γῆς· τὸν ἄρτον ἡμῶν τὸν ἐπιούσιον δὸς ἡμῖν
>   σήμερον, καὶ ἄφες ἡμῖν τὴν **ὀφειλὴν** ἡμῶν ὡς καὶ ἡμεῖς
>   ἀφίεμεν τοῖς ὀφειλέταις ἡμῶν, καὶ μὴ εἰσενέγκῃς ἡμᾶς εἰς

πειρασμόν, ἀλλὰ ῥῦσαι ἡμᾶς ἀπὸ τοῦ πονηροῦ· ὅτι σοῦ ἐστιν
ἡ δύναμις καὶ ἡ δόξα εἰς τοὺς αἰῶνας.

UBS: Πάτερ ἡμῶν ὁ ἐν τοῖς **οὐρανοῖς**, ἁγιασθήτω τὸ ὄνομά σου·
ἐλθέτω ἡ βασιλεία σου· γενηθήτω τὸ θέλημά σου, ὡς ἐν οὐ
'ρανῷ καὶ ἐπὶ γῆς· τὸν ἄρτον ἡμῶν τὸν ἐπιούσιον δὸς ἡμῖν
σήμερον· καὶ ἄφες ἡμῖν τὰ **ὀφειλήματα** ἡμῶν, ὡς καὶ ἡμεῖς
ἀφήκαμεν τοῖς ὀφειλέταις ἡμῶν· καὶ μὴ εἰσενέγκῃς ἡμᾶς εἰς
πειρασμόν, ἀλλὰ ῥῦσαι ἡμᾶς ἀπὸ τοῦ πονηροῦ.]

I have highlighted the words that indicate some difference between the *Didache* text and that in Matthew. As one can see, the differences are minimal. The *Didache* has the singular "heaven" and "debt" while the Matthew text has those words in the plural. There is also a slight change in tense of the Greek word for "forgive." No differences, however, affect the meaning conveyed in the prayer in the least.

There is an addition at the end of the prayer in the *Didache* that is not in our modern critical text since it is not in the earliest Greek manuscripts of Matthew. It is similar to but shorter than the addition familiar to all Christians that is found in the later Byzantine addition to the prayer (see textual apparatus in UBS or Nestle for the details). While initially this addition to the prayer in *Didache* may appear to affirm that later Byzantine reading, the truth may be just the opposite. Note that this doxological ascription appears later in the *Didache* in almost the same form and is appended to the Eucharistic prayers in 9:2,3,4 and 10:2,4,5. It is very similar to a common ending to prayers in the Jewish liturgy that survive until today.[62] A better explanation is that the *Didache* is an early witness to the tendency of scribes to add doxological ascriptions, which only increased in later times when the doxological ascription crystallized and became part of the received text in the Middle Ages in Byzantine areas (Western/Latin texts also omit the doxology along with Alexandrian family texts).

Another apparent citation from Matthew is found in the section of the *Didache* where the eucharist is being explained. The Didachist supports his point that only believers should partake of the eucharist in the following manner:

9:5 (And) let no one eat or drink from your eucharist
except those baptized in the name of the Lord,
for also the Lord has said concerning this:
"Do not give what is holy to the dogs."

[*Didache* of Didache 9:5: Μὴ δῶτε τὸ ἅγιον τοῖς κυσί.
UBS text of Matt. 7:6: Μὴ δῶτε τὸ ἅγιον τοῖς κυσίν.]

The issue of the form of the text citation is fairly simple. The texts are identical, unless one fusses about the "movable *nu*" in Matthew! Authority for this saying is traced back by directly to the "Lord." Occasionally, this title is used in a general sense in the *Didache*, but as it does here, it often clearly refers to Jesus (see also 6:2; 8:2; 11:2, 4, 8; 12:1; 14:1; 15:4; 16:1, 8). It is not the "form" issue but the "hermeneutical" issue that confronts us in this text. An ancient or modern reader of the Sermon on the Mount would probably not think of "closed communion" for believers as the original intention of this Dominical saying in Matt. 7:6. Does that indicate that the Didachist has ripped this saying out of its original Matthean context and applied it wrongly to the issue of correct participation in the Eucharistic observance? Proponents of the non-use of the Gospels by the Apostolic Fathers have no problem here. They affirm that this saying was either taken from the oral tradition or from a Jewish milieu and was used by the Didachist in this way for his purpose and also by the "Matthean" author there for his purpose.[63] Is there another way to approach this?

The context of this saying appears in the Sermon on the Mount at the end of Jesus' warning against hypocritical judging of others (7:1-5) and precedes a pericope on prayer (7:6-11). Matthew 7:1-5 comprise a strong warning against harsh and wrongful discernment. To balance that warning, Jesus in verse six then gives what could very well have been a proverbial Jewish saying to teach that there is such a thing as correct discernment about those who in reality are "dogs" and "pigs." That is the legitimate connection between 7:1-5 and 7:6 and the commentators bear this out.[64] If this be the case, the Didachist is stating that it is not a harsh act to deny the eucharist to unbelievers but it is a wise act of discernment. As a matter of fact, the leaders of the assembly have a moral and spiritual responsibility to do so. While this verse was not originally given in Matthew to limit participation in the eucharist to believers, the Didachist's use of it is consistent with the way Jesus used it to make His own point in the Sermon on the Mount.

A Proposal about *Didache* and Matthew

I mentioned earlier that one way of handling the divergences between *Didache* and Matthew is that the Didachist may not have been quoting Matthew literally but rather adapting it to suit his purposes. There is another way to accommodate both the similarities and the differences between these two texts. How can we affirm that the *Didache* knew and used "Matthew" and at the same time recognize why there is not exact equivalence between the two?

I have found the approach to this problem proposed by Andre Tuilier quite convincing.[65] I will try to summarize his argument as follows. Tuilier believes that the evidence of 8:2 and 15:3, 4 is quite convincing that the Didachist utilized some written account that he titles, "The Gospel of the Lord" (το εὐαγγελιον τοῦ κυρίου). Can we know what that "gospel" was? Tuilier brings forward the evidence of Papias' oft-discussed statement preserved by Eusebius that "Matthew arranged the sayings (λογία) of the Lord in the Hebrew/Aramaic (ἑβραΐδι) language and others interpreted (ἑρμηνεύσεν) them as they could." Tuilier argues that it was a Greek translation of those Aramaic *logia* that the Didachist had and from which he quoted. It is well known that the Greek verb ἑρμήνευσεν often was used for "translating" from one language to another rather than simply "interpreting" within the same language.[66]

Tuilier proposes that Matthew arranged the logia of the Lord around 45 C.E.; someone translated it into Greek by 55-60; and the Gospel of Matthew in its finished form appeared by 65-70. Therefore, sometime between 55-65 the Didachist quoted the "Gospel of the Lord" in his handbook. As befits the meaning of λογία, this was a "sayings" Gospel. It is noteworthy that only sayings of Jesus are quoted in the *Didache*. No mention of his deeds is made.

Tuilier further develops his proposal by identifying the "Gospel of the Lord" with what scholars for years have referred to as the "Q" source. He provides a stemma tracing not only the above proposed development of Matthew's "Sayings Gospel" but also how Luke utilized it along with Mark (60 C.E.) in composing his own Gospel (65 C.E.).[67] It is interesting to note that Tuilier does not propose that "Matthew" used his own *logia* plus Mark to compose his final version, but that he drew on other oral tradition about the Lord's deeds combined with the Greek "Gospel of the Lord" to complete his masterpiece. Tuilier also discusses how Tatian's *Diatessaron* utilized not only the four canonical Gospels but also the Greek "Gospel of the Lord" in writing his own famous harmony around 170.

Tuilier's identifying of the "Gospel of the Lord" as the lost "Q" and his reconstruction of the synoptic developments and his explanation of Tatian's procedure are issues that cannot detain us here. I do suggest, however, that Tuilier's proposal about an earlier form of a Greek "Matthew" as identical to a Greek translation of the Aramaic logia has succeeded in addressing the question of the relationship between Matthew and the *Didache* in a most satisfying manner. It very happily explains both the similarities and the differences between *Didache* and canonical Matthew. It also shows as unnecessary the idea that the Didachist was simply quoting free-floating oral sayings of Jesus – an idea that is difficult to maintain in light of 8:2 and 15:3, 4.

Another happy implication of Tuilier's proposal is that it allows us to more comfortably locate the writing of the *Didache* earlier than demanded by a "post-canonical Matthew" dating (after 70 C.E., or even later by most scholars). This earlier dating of *Didache* is more in line with what nearly everyone recognizes as the book's primitive theology, its simple church leadership, its traveling apostles and prophets, its lack of mentioning persecution, its lack of warning against aberrant doctrine, and its lack of knowledge of Paul – all of which are part of the picture of church life that emerges in the book.

So, in answer to our earlier question, "Did the *Didache* know and use the Gospel of Matthew?," the answer is a resounding "yes." But if Tuilier is correct, and I think there is good reason to conclude that he is, then the Didachist cites a version of "Matthew" that was earlier than the canonical Matthew that has come down to us.

Use of Non-Canonical Material

While more could be written about the *Didache*'s use of the Old and New Testament citations and allusions, enough examples have been mentioned to give evidence of the author's agreement with the broad scope of general NT theology and practice as well as his fashioning of specific NT verses for his own specific purposes. Now some brief attention should be given to the question of whether or not the Didachist refers to non-canonical literature, and if he does, how he uses that material.

It would be appropriate at this point to address the question of whether the *Didache* utilizes an existing non-canonical Jewish "Two ways" document in framing chapters 1-5. I will postpone that question, however, until the next chapter when we look at how the Didachist presents the "two ways" in those chapters.

Early in the *Didache* we encounter a familiar saying that is expressed in an unfamiliar way to Christian ears. There we meet with what has often been called the "Negative Golden Rule." *Didache* 1:2b states: "As many things as you wish not to happen to you, likewise, do not do to another." While this is certainly similar to Jesus' statement in Matt. 7:12, in that familiar verse it is expressed positively. There is, however, a pre-Christian history to this piece of ethical advice. Tobit's advice to his son in 4:15 "And what you hate, do not do to anyone" expresses a similar thought. Furthermore, the famous dictum of Hillel to the inquiring Gentile in Talmud *Babli Shabbat* 31a also sounds very similar to Didache 1:2b: "That which is harmful to you, do not do to another." Did the Didachist deliberately alter the Dominical saying in accord with Jewish tradition or could this be an example of a genuine agraphon—an unwritten saying of Jesus? We simply do not know, but we should recognize that this is a further example of the very Jewish character of the Didache, even in its Christian dress.

One of the most perplexing statements in the Didache has been often noted by scholars who have pondered over the source that the Didachist cites. It comes at the end of chapter one, concluding a previously noted passage that encourages giving, with many sayings similar to the Sermon on the Mount (1:3-5). Didache 1:6 then states, "But also, concerning this, on the other hand, it has been said: 'Let your alms sweat in your hands, until you know to whom you should give it'." This appears to be a warning against indiscriminate almsgiving, with the worthiness of the potential alms-receiver as being very important to recognize before the alms-giver acts. Many commentators have noted a similar sentiment expressed in Sirach 12:1: "If you do good, know to whom you do it, and you will be thanked for your good deeds" (ἐὰν εὖ ποιῇς γνῶθι τίνι ποιεῖς καὶ ἔσται χάρις τοῖς ἀγαθοῖς σου). The wording of Sirach, however, is quite different from the way in which this dictum is quoted. The Didachist does appear to be quoting something because he uses the "citation formula" word εἴρηται—"it has been said").

I suggest that he did use *Sirach* but not in the way he is often understood to have done. In one of the most brilliant examples of linguistic detective work I have ever read, the Dead Sea Scrolls scholar Patrick Skehan has shown in light of a Hebrew copy of *Sirach* found in the Cairo Geniza, that it is possible that an ancient scribe mistook a Hebrew word for "truth" for the same initialed word for "sweat."[68] This misunderstanding of the original Hebrew text of *Sirach* could have lead to the strange translation into Greek that we read in the *Didache* which utilizes the Old Greek version exclusively.

There is one more piece of linguistic phenomena then helps us to see *why* the Didachist quoted this strange text from a non-canonical book – something that he apparently does not do anywhere else in his work. The introduction to the quotation runs like this in Greek: ἀλλὰ καὶ περὶ τούτου δὲ εἴρηται. The strong adversative conjunction ἀλλὰ plus the conjunction καὶ and then later another milder adversative conjunction δὲ each combine together to make a rather involved Greek construction. Elsewhere in the *Didache*, the adversative ἀλλὰ always introduces a strong contrast with what has gone before (see 2:5; 2:7; 3:9; 4:9; 8:2; 16:1). I suggest that the same strong adversative idea is found here. What the Didachist is doing is to contrast the generous giving commanded by Jesus with the "tight-fisted" attitude commended by Sirach in 12:1-7, which is worth reading in its context to note its further pessimistic tone about giving to unworthy people. In addition, this verse's advice as it is quoted is totally opposite the spirit and practice of giving that is commended elsewhere in the book. Note particularly the advice in 4:8: "You will not turn away the one in need; but you will share together all things with your brother and you will not say that such things are your own; for, if you (pl.) are partners in what is immortal, how much more [are you partners] in the mortal things?"

My conclusion is that the Didachist actually did utilize a non-canonical work and even quoted it. But he did so, not to utilize it as a positive witness to what he had just taught, but as a negative hostile witness to a behavior which he intends for his readers to avoid.

There are other possible echoes of *Sirach* in the book. Some of these were noted as early as Bryennios' volume.[69] He thought that *Sirach* 2:4 could be seen reflected in *Didache* 3:10; *Sirach* 4:5 could be seen in *Didache* 3:10; and Sirach 4:31 could be cited in *Didache* 4:6. The last of these references is the clearest example of a citation from that book of proverbial wisdom. This is consistent with the pattern of wisdom teaching reflecting *Sirach* that was noted earlier. The Didachist was not alone among early Christian writers who looked for guidance to this book that did not make it into the Hebrew canon.

Summary and Conclusions

We have briefly surveyed the way in which the Didachist used the canonical scriptures to transmit to Gentile believers what he believed was the teaching of the Twelve Apostles. A few observations on particularly how he does that now follow.

1. The Didachist, while sometimes creatively re-arranging canonical material, knew that authority lay in those scriptures, not in himself. There are no attempts to present himself as a channel of divine revelation. He looked to the

inspired scriptures of the Old Testament and to the words of Jesus for help in transmitting that "teaching."

2. The Didachist was aware of Matthew's Gospel (in its earliest form) and used it freely. He did not hesitate to adapt some of the words of Jesus by arranging them in an order to effectively argue his point of ethical paranesis. It appears, however, that even when he did re-arrange material, he always remained consistent with the authorial intent of those passages.

3. The Didachist used various sections of the OT, especially the "Law" and the "Prophets," although not extensively. It appears that he knew and used that form of the Greek text which we know as the Septuagint. The LXX, as was the case with most of the NT writers and the vast majority of Patristic writers, was his Bible, along with the words of Jesus in the "Gospel of the Lord."

4. From the OT passages that he used, it does not appear that the Didachist employed the allegorical method that became popular in the early second century, as is exemplified by the Epistle of Barnabas. While he did not hesitate to see a change from literal sacrifices under the Old Covenant to spiritual sacrifices under the New, in this he was consistent with the practice of New Testament writers, although he was unaware of most of those writings. He follows, therefore, a redemptive historical hermeneutic in seeing progression in meaning, but not an authorially intended allegorizing of the OT passages so that they had a hidden meaning different than the historical grammatical meaning that they conveyed when they were written.

5. The paradigmatic pattern of *citations, quotations, allusions* and *echoes* mentioned earlier as ways in which NT writers referenced the Old appears also to be the pattern in which the Didachist used the authoritative scripture available to him. Examples of each of those ways of referring to authoritative scripture can be found in the little book. By citing authoritative scripture, the *Didache* accomplished what it set out to do—to provide a faithful record to the Gentiles of the teaching of the apostles.

Chapter Six

The Two Ways of the *Didache*

In the next few chapters we will attempt to survey the actual contents of the *Didache*, but as we begin it is also necessary to mention one more matter of controversy and academic debate. It has to do with what source(s), if any, that the Didachist utilized in the writing of chapters 1-6, or at least chapters 1-5. I mentioned in the introduction that issues of source and redaction criticism have dominated *Didache* research for over fifty years and that such issues will not dominate my own treatment of the book. I am concerned that the overall message of the book has often been lost amid the endless discussion of sources and editors that have been proposed in discussions of its compositional history. Thus it is necessary that we mention why these issues will not control our presentation.

Scholars for years have noticed that *Didache* 1-5 develops the theme of the "two ways." 1:1 opens with: "There are two ways: one of **life** and one of **death**! And there is a great difference between the two ways." Later he concludes the first part of this section with the summary statement, "This is the way of life!" (4:14b). He then launches the second section this way: "The way of death, on the other hand, is this" (5:1, 2). There have been a number of efforts to claim that the Didachist adapted an existing Jewish "two ways" ethical treatise to his "Jewish Christian" purposes.[70] There has even been an ingenious effort to actually reconstruct the content of such a proposed Greek "Two Ways" treatise by utilizing the Latin *Doctrina Apostolorum* as the key to this supposed source.[71] I deeply respect the scholarship of those involved in this re-construction, but I also am deeply concerned that it rests far too much on conjecture than solid evidence. With the publication of the Dead Sea Scrolls, there have also been efforts to find parallels to the thought in the *Didache*. This is particularly true because the early chapters of *Didache* exhibit some reflections of such an ethical treatise in the Community Rule of that sect.[72]

However, after initially being quite positive about the possibility of the Di-dachist's adaptation of a Jewish document to his purpose, I have become convinced that the relationship has been greatly overdrawn. Such an effort, in my opinion, suffers from what has come to be called "parallelomania"—the unjustified effort to see parallels and borrowings from one body of literature to another based on either anachronistic or very slim analogies between the two.

The simple fact of the matter is that no clear example of a Jewish "two ways" document from the period antedating the *Didache* has ever been found! It is easy to postulate the existence of such a document's existence, but it has been hard to find such a thing. A careful *Didache* scholar recognized this when he wrote about attempts to make the Qumran material a source for the *Didache*.

> One must not lose the unique perspective that the comparison between the *Manual of Discipline* from Qumran and the different forms of the Christian *duae viae* brings concerning the *dualistic framework* (which is absent in the *Didache*!) and concerning the general literary genre of instruction which places side by side a list of virtue and a list of vices; but in the detail of content and vocabulary, resemblances are missing.[73]

It is interesting to note that just three years after *Didache*'s publication, the great scholar, Benjamin Warfield warned against any effort to argue for a Jewish "two ways" *vorlage*, in light of the meager evidence of such ever existing.[74] I challenge any interested readers to actually read "The Community Rule" (1QS 3:13-4:26) and find there anything that would make one think of *Didache* 1-5 if they had not been preconditioned to do so. In my opinion, the only similarity in the two documents is the word "two." The Scroll speaks of "two" angels – one of darkness and one of light and how men are ruled by one of "two" spirits. This is parallel to the much later rabbinic concept of the two inclinations in man —the *yetzer hara* and the *yetzer hatov*.[75] However, it bears very little resemblance to the *Didache* description of the two ways—except again in the word "two." Such language about "two" angels or inclinations also characterizes the similar chapters in *Barnabas* 18-20 and in the *Doctrina Apostolorum*. In my opinion, this elaboration of the simplicity expressed in the *Didache*'s rehearsal of the "two ways" points to the secondary character of these documents. I realize that I am going against a large scholarly guild in questioning this postulating of a Jewish ethical "two ways" treatise. But there are scholars later than Warfield who have voiced similar doubts. Among them is the German scholar Michaelis in his article in the *Theological Dictionary of the New Testament*.[76]

Not only do we not have a copy of this hypothetical Jewish "two ways" document for Gentile proselytes, we have no written source describing or referring to such a document. We certainly acknowledge that it is impossible to prove the non-existence of something. Because of this, there may very well have actually existed a pre-Christian Jewish ethical treatise in something like a "two ways" format. Perhaps, however, there is another possibility that should also be considered. Many scholars have suggested that the *Didache* may have been composed in two stages. The first would be a version written in the early days of the initial influx of Gentile believers into the Antioch church, witnessed to in Acts 11:19 ff.—probably not much later than 40 C.E. That could have been the document that some feel is represented by the *Doctrina Apostolorum*—a document lacking the evangelical section in chapter one and the "Gospel" references later in the book. Then, when the Greek "Gospel of the Lord" emerged between 45-55 C.E., the Didachist could have added those "gospel" references and thus we would have the "finished" *Didache* by the 60's. If this be the case, we do have solid ovidence of a prior "two ways"document – within the text of the *Didache* itself! I realize that I have not proved my case for this proposal, but it has as much plausibility as proposing the existence of a source document for which we have no clear evidence.

Until there is more concrete evidence of its existence—apart from a Medieval Latin document—it is safer to look for the antecedents of the "two ways" genre in other Jewish sources and patterns of teaching. And such examples can be found in abundance. It should be noted that the "two ways" ethical pattern is very Jewish and has deep roots in Jewish Scripture. Consider Deut. 30:19: "I call heaven and earth to witness against you today, that I have set before you life and death." Psalm 1 graphically describes the two ways with their contrasting results. The wisdom literature of the Hebrew Bible is replete with this comparison and contrast. Consider Proverbs 1-9 with its comparison of the "Way of Wisdom" with the "Way of Folly." Jeremiah was sent by the Lord to say to the people: "Behold I set before you the way of life and the way of death" (21:8). In a roughly contemporary text, the *Apocalypse of Baruch*, the author states that the Lord said to the people, "Behold I have set before you life and death" (19:1). But it is not necessary that suggest that the *Didache* actually quoted any of these Jewish documents. He may only have been following in a very long train of thought and expression. And, in my opinion, it is even more risky to propose that he Christianized a hypothetical document which we do not have!

It seems much more reasonable to see both the *Didache* and the Hebrew scriptures as employing a literary pattern ingrained in pre-Christian Jewish thinking and expression. The evidence for that pattern in pre-Christian sources is very evident, as has been seen. That same ethical and literary pattern then served as a paradigm for the Didachist to employ, expand and develop in his Jewish Christian ethical treatise. If there was dependence on a specific source, it makes much more sense to see it as inspiration derived from another Jewish teacher who was also thoroughly versed in the Hebrew "two ways" thinking. Since his teaching inspired so much else in the *Didache*, could not his words, like the following, inspired the Didachist? "Enter by the narrow gate. For the gate is wide and the way is easy that leads to destruction, and those who enter by it are many. For the gate is narrow and the way is hard that leads to life, and those who find it are few" (Matt. 7:13, 14). Sometimes things may be much simpler than we try to make them.

The Development of the Two Ways Teaching
(ch. 1-6)

One of the most prolific authors on the *Didache* has been Aaron Milavec. After contributing a number of articles on subjects related to the *Didache*, in 2003 he published his *magnum opus*, a nearly thousand page commentary which treated the text and many issues related to it.[77] In the same year a much shorter work by Milavec also appeared that summarized his larger commentary.[78] Milavec argues that the *Didache* is independent of the canonical Gospels and dates from 50-70 A.D. More creatively, he offers an origination hypothesis for the writing of the *Didache* that is unique among the many authors who have written on it. Milavec affirms strongly the unity of the *Didache* over against the hypotheses of its many sources and its original orality prior to its written function. He then traces through the book what he believes is the consistent development of a systematic training program embodied in its contents. Its purpose was to mold and to shape the life of a convert from paganism into the new faith taught by Jesus and experienced by his followers.

Milavec has thought long and hard about this book, and his penchant for unique interpretations should not cause his readers to be put off and thus overlook the keen insights that he brings to the meaning of so many debated passages. But it is not his interpretation of individual texts that makes Milavec an engaging discussion partner. It is his effort to stress the overall unity of the book that should be welcomed by those of us who are weary of what the source critics have done to this little book. Personally, I do not think that Milavec has sealed his case for the original oral character of the document. Nor do I think he has proven that it embodies a training program conducted by one mentor and his disciple. I do believe, however, that he has uncovered the book's overall unity – something that has been missing in the authors who have often engaged in atomistic analyses of this and that section – and have often missed the proverbial forest by examining so closely the trees.

Until someone offers a better approach to the book as a whole, Milavec's massive treatment will be, if not the last word, at least the standard which others must emulate. You may disagree with him, but you cannot ignore him. From the perspective of my own origination hypothesis—that the *Didache* was intended to be a catechetical book and was used that way from its emergence—I find much that is welcome in his work. In the chapters to come, he will be a welcome dialogue partner in exploring "the way of the *Didache*," especially in its early chapters. Therefore, with Milavec often at my elbow, I offer the following summary of the way that the Didachist outlines for the new life of a believer in God's servant, Jesus.

An Overall Analysis of the *Didache*

The *Didache* itself indicates that it is not simply a pastiche of similar but disjointed elements. The discourse markers that the Didachist employs indicate that his work is divided into two main sections. The first is marked off by the expression "way of life" in 1:2 and the expression "way of death" in 5:1-2. Further markers are the expressions, "This is the teaching" in 1:3a and "this is the way of life" in 4:14b. These expressions serve an *inclusio* function in framing the first part of the book. Thus, chapters 1-5 are intended to embody as a self-contained literary unit the teaching that was to be given to new believer before his or her baptism. This is clear from 7:1, "After you have said all these things beforehand, immerse in the name of the Father and of the Son and of the Holy Spirit in flowing water." "These things" can only refer to the teaching embodied previously in chapters 1-5.

The second main section of the book (chapters 6-16) consists of instructions about how the young believer is to relate to life in the public worship and ministry of the church. The similar expression "you will be perfect" in 6:2 and "unless you are perfected" in 16:2 again serve as an inclusio to frame the second section. Thus, the last chapter is not simply an eschatological appendix but is deliberately crafted to advance the overall plan of the Didachist. Within that frame in the second section, the Didachist employs the discourse marker "and concerning" (περὶ δὲ) a total of five times, each time to introduce a new topic for the catechumen to learn about and in which to participate. These are: 1) Food to eat and to avoid (6:3); 2) Baptism and how it is administered (7:1); 3) The eucharist (9:1) of cup and bread (9:3); and 4) The role of apostles and prophets (11:3). This discourse marker function of the περὶ δε can be seen also in First Corinthians 7:1, 25; 8:1, 12:1; 16:1, 12 and in First Thessalonians 4:9 and 5:1. It is probably too much to conclude on the basis of this usage a Pauline influence, since the Didachist does not indicate knowledge of Paul's writings in any other way. One possible thought, however, should be considered. Paul used the occurrences of περὶ δὲ to enumerate his successive answers to the questions that the Corinthians had asked him about in a previous letter (7:1). Could its use by the Didachist also imply that the subjects he addresses were ones that local congregations had asked him about in previous communications? Thus, chapters 6-11 ff. could be providing guidance by answering queries that had arisen in the churches within the circle of the Didachist's influence.

Chapter 6:3, therefore, with its mitigated command regarding kosher eating thus would be separate from chapters 1:1-6:2. It also serves, however, as a bridge to the following material due to its being the first example in the περὶ δὲ schematic. The Didachist desired that this point of guidance about eating food should be included in the teaching to be given to young believers. The material in 7:1ff, as important as it was to the corporate life of the body, was not part of the individual instruction that was given in ch. 1-6. The final chapter contains an earnest exhortation, therefore, to "seek what is appropriate for your souls" in light of the coming of the Lord. That which is appropriate would primarily be the pre-baptismal instruction of chapters 1-6 but also include the "church" teaching in chapters 7-15 that would cover post-baptismal experiences. See, for example, the exhortation in 9:5, "And let no one eat or drink from your thanksgiving meal except those baptized in the name of the Lord."

An Overview of *Didache* 1-6

Returning now to our focus on *Didache* 1-6, the order of the topics is as follows, with my own modifications to Milavec's outline:

1. Two Ways of Life (1:1, 2);
2. Two Rules of Giving (1:3-6);
3. Six New Commandments (2:1-2);
4. Five Speech Infractions (2:3-5);
5. Five Forbidden Dispositions (2:6-7);
6. Five "Fences" (3:1-6);
7. Five Positive Virtues (3:7-10);
8. Five Congregational Precepts (4:1-4);
9. Four Guidelines for Giving (4:5-8);
10. Three Household Rules (4:9-11);
11. Three Solemn Admonitions (4:12-14);
12. Forty Foul Actions (5:1, 2).
13. Warning Against Innovators (6:1, 2).[79]

The Title(s) of the *Didache*

It is difficult to affirm with confidence that either of the two titles was part of the first century work. The short one, "The Teaching of the Apostles" (Διδαχὴ τῶν ἀποστόλων), was written with red ink in the Jerusalem manuscript. The longer one, "The Teaching of the Lord Through the Twelve Apostles to the Gentiles" (Διδαχὴ κυρίου διὰ τῶν δώδεκα ἀποστόλων τοῖς ἔθνεσιν) opens the first line of the manuscript. Apart from these titles, however, the expression "twelve apostles" does not appear elsewhere in the body of the book. When "apostles" are mentioned in the book, as in 11:3-6, the term refers to wandering charismatics, for it would be difficult to see how any of the Twelve would be limited to two days in their stay (11:5), or would be asking wrongly for money (11:6). The Didachist simply refers to the "teaching" (1:3) as being given by "the Lord" (9:3). Milavec cncludes, "The distinct possibility remains, therefore, that 'twelve apostles' was introduced only at the point when apostolic authorship was recognized as an absolute necessity for any work seeking inclusion in the canon of approved books."[80]

The Two-Fold Command

While the responsibilities of loving God and loving your fellow man can certainly be found in Judaism, the joining of the two texts, Deut. 6:5 and Lev. 19:18, as they are joined in 1:2, is not found in non-Christian Jewish texts before this time. The synoptic Gospels assign such coupling to Jesus (Mat. 22:37-39; Mark 12:30, 31; Luke 10:27). The way that the Didachist employs Deut. 6:5, however, is not in the form familiarly known as the *Shema*. It mentions "God", not "Lord" (see LXX) and the description of Him is as "the one who made you," not the covenantal language of Deut. 6. This expression, however, would be appropriate for Gentiles, who were not in any covenant relationship to the "Lord" but were still created by "God."

This uniquely "Christian " language right at the beginning of the two ways section points up another of the reasons it is difficult to see chapters 1-5 as some pre-Christian Jewish "two ways treatise." Not only here but in many other places expressions are used that are more familiar in a (Jewish) Christian context than in a Jewish context. Consider 2:7: "Don't hate anyone, reprove some, pray for some, love some more than your soul." Can that sentiment be found in pre-Christian Judaism? The accepting of whatever happens to you as "good" (3:10), although similar to Sirach 2:4, differs greatly in the language used. Providence was taught in Judaism, but the accepting of things as "good" is a Christian expression rather than a Jewish one (cf. Rom. 8:28). The following verses in the *Didache* also seem more suited to Christian than to Jewish "talk." "My child, remember the one who preaches to you the words of God, for where Lordship is proclaimed, there is the Lord" (4:1). "Seek out the presence of the saints, to find support in their words" (4.2). "You are sharers in imperishable things, how much more in the perishable?" (4.8b). "Confess your sins in the ἐκκλησία"—not in the συναγωγη! (4.14). Also, the description of the Holy Spirit preparing people simply sounds more like a Christian than a Jewish expression (4:10). This is not intended to imply that the morality of Christianity is different than that of Judaism. The difference is in the manner of expression, not in the superiority or inferiority of one to the other.

Before we return to the actual content of the *Didache*, I do think it is also appropriate to note some important matters that are *not* discussed in *Didache* 1-5. The absence of these things in a Jewish text intended for Gentile converts simply appears very odd to me. While plenty of commands and rules are issued, there is no explicit mention of the first four commandments. There is no mention of Sabbath observance, circumcision, or the dietary laws. The absence of the first five commandments and those three prominent badges of Jewish identity would be unthinkable in a Jewish manual intended to introduce Judaism to Gentile proselytes. Someone may respond that the above Christian verses were added and the prominent Jewish badges were omitted when the text was adopted by the Didachist. My response is that if all problems with a theory are explained as redactions then it may be time to take another hard look at the theory.

Much has been written about the so-called "negative" Golden Rule that finds expression in 1:2b, "As many things as you wish not to happen to you, likewise, do not do to another." Antecedents can be found in *Tobit* 4:15 and also in the famous story of Hillel, Shammai, and the Gentile (*Shabbat* 31a). Although it does not appear in the NT in this form, a variant reading adds it to the "apostolic decree in Acts 15:29. While Jesus' famous saying in *Matt.* 7:12 and *Luke* 7:31 is expressed positively, Jesus could also have used the other form at times. Possibly it appeared that way in "The Gospel of the Lord," which the Didachist used elsewhere and thus he cites it in that form here.

Two Rules of Giving (1:3, 4; 4:5-8)

The following paragraph (1:3-2:1) is often referred to as the "evangelical section" since it is very similar to Jesus' teaching in Matthew's "Sermon on the Mount" (ch. 5-7) and in Luke's "Sermon on the Plain" (ch. 6). The initial stress on praying for enemies and turning the cheek may have had reference to the new spiritual "enemies" that had developed in the young convert's life because of his new faith. The advice was very helpful in maintaining a non-violent reaction to an abusive family situation.[81]

The issue of giving is taken up near the beginning and near the end of the intial section of chapters 1-4. The first instruction on giving (1:4)[82] is in the present imperative mode in the Greek. The second command (4:5-8) is presented in the future tense, called an "imperatival future."[83] Since this use of the imperative is largely confined in the NT to the quotation of OT commands, grammarians tend to thnk that the imperatival future may be more emphatic rather than general. In the *Didache* the context of the second command on giving is the church fellowship and the importance of sharing with brothers and sisters in the Lord. Thus the future would express the time when the new convert would be fully accepted in the congregation after his baptism. The first rule for giving expressed in the imperative, however, was intended for immediate implementation. Developing the giving habit of mind in chapter one could then better lead to the more emphatic command in chapter four.

Six New Commandments (2:1, 2)

In this section of firm and straightforward commands, the Didachist omits the first five commandments. Some are implied in other commands (1:2; 2:3), while others, like the Sabbath command, had been superseded by the command to gather on the Lord's Day (14:1). Milavec thinks that the omission of the fifth command to honor parents may reflect the familial situation of pagan converts experiencing conflict from parents for their new faith. They were to honor God as their true Father (1:5; 9:2-3; 10:2).[84]

The latter five commands of the Decalogue are reiterated in 2:2, expressed in the familiar negative particle (ου in Greek) plus the future imperative of the prohibited verb. The Didachist also adds six new ones that appear to be in some ways elaborations of the five. They come in three pairs. The first two condemn pedophilia and illicit sex: "you will not corrupt children; you will not have illicit sex." Pedophilia was so foreign to Jewish practice that it is not even mentioned in the Torah. Yet it was common in the Gentile world from which these converts came. "Illicit sex" is the verb form of the noun πορνεία, a general word for just that, "illicit sex." In addition to the obvious act of adultery, all forms of prohibited sexual relations are here proscribed, such as incest and prostitution (Lev. 18:6-16; 21:9). The second pair prohibits magic and the making of potions (φαρ μακεύειν), an activity that must have been linked with magic. The last pair pertain to abortion and infanticide: "you will not murder a child by means of abortion, nor you will kill one that has been born." These practices were widely regarded in the pagan world as normal means of family limitation.[85] This firm opposition to accepted practices in the Roman world came to be regarded as one of the chef differences that people noticed in the early Christians. This is the earliest reference in Christian literature that explicitly forbids what was implicit in scripture.

Five Speech Sins, Five Evil Dispositions and Five Fences (2:3-3:6)

In 2:3-5, the Didachist warns against five "sins of the tongue" which echo many of the warnings about the tongue in both the testaments. This is followed by the forbidding of five "sins of the attitude" in 2:6, 7. The command not to hate anyone is followed immediately by some positive counsel that balances the command against hatred: "but some you will reprove, and for others you will pray, and some you will love more than your soul" (2:7b).

This is standard Christian paranesis that can be found in many Christian works, both within and without the canon. What follows in chapter three, however, is framed in a way that was familiar to Jews of the Second temple Period. There are five warninmgs against certain behaviors that are then followed by actuions that the forbidden acts will lead to if they are not forsaken. This is so striking that I quote the entire passage of 3:1-6 in analytical form which will help the reader see the point being made more clearly.

3:1 My child, flee from every evil
     and from everything like it.

3:2 [1] Do not become angry,
          for anger leads to murder;
          nor be envious,
          nor be contentious,
          nor be hot-headed,
          for, from all these, murders are born.

3:3 [2] My child, do not become lustful,
          for lust leads to illicit sex;
          nor use foul speech,
          nor be one who lifts up the eyes,
          for, from all these, adulteries are born.

3:4 [3] My child, do not practice divination,
          since this leads to idolatry;
          nor be an enchanter,
          nor be an astrologer,
          nor be a magician,
          nor even wish to see nor hear these things,
          for, from all these, idolatry is born.

3:5 [4] My child, do not become false,

since falsehood leads to theft;
nor be a lover of money,
nor be a seeker of glory,
for, from all these, thefts are born.

3:6 [5] My child, do not become a grumbler,
since this leads to blasphemy;
nor be a self-pleaser,
nor be evil-minded,
for, from all these, blasphemies are born.[86]

The structure of this passage is fraught with features that would be familiar to Jewish readers. It has already been noted that the repeated addresses to "my child" (τεκνον μου) echoes wisdom literature such as Proverbs, where a similar expression appears fifteen times and also Sirach, where the exactly same expression appears nineteen times.

The second characteristic in this passage that finds abundant parallels in Jewish literature is the practice of constructing a fence around the Torah to keep one from coming too close to the commands and break them. For example, in *Avot de Rabbi Nathan* 17a, the rabbis taught that Adam was the first to construct a fence around God's command not to eat from the tree by telling Eve that "we should not touch it" (see Gen. 3:3). In a later manual for training rabbinic disciples, *Derek Erez Zuta*, a number of additional "fences" strikingly similar to *Didache* 3:1-6 are offered (*DEZ* 2:7; 3:6). Recent scholarship has warned us to be careful of anachronistic citing of later works of rabbinic literature as if they were legitimate background for first century texts.[87] There are other examples, however, of this fence building in the Second Temple *Testaments of the Twelve Patriarchs*, especially *T. Judah* 14:1 and 19:1. There the author employs the same verb, "leads to" (ὁδηγεῖ), that is used five times in *Didache* 3:2-6.[88]

But we do not need to travel outside the boundaries of Jewish Christian literature to find similar examples of "building a fence" around the Torah commandments to keep people from breaking them. One could conclude that a very similar approach was taken by Jesus in the Sermon on the Mount. Following his statement that his followers' righteousness should exceed that of the Pharisees (Matt. 5:17, 18), Jesus mentions a number of specific Torah prohibitions, especially those directed against murder and adultery. Jesus warns that these outward sins really are no worse than the corresponding attitudes of anger and lust (Matt. 5:21-30). It is possible that his warnings also could be framed in the following ways.

My child, do not become angry, for anger leads to murder.
My child, do not become lustful, for lust leads to illicit sex.
(*Didache* 3:2, 3)

Five Positive Virtues (3:7-10)

The Didachist follows these firm admonitions against destructive deeds with a positive affirmation of good practices to follow. In this way, he follows a time honored method of showing what behaviors need to be "put off" and then what needs to be "put on" in their place (cf. Eph. 4:22-24).

The qualities of meekness, long-suffering, mercy, and gentleness seem to echo Christian language as that enunciated by Jesus in a number of places. The quotation in 3:8, "But be meek, since the meek will inherit the earth" is one of the beatitudes in Matt. 5:5. The wording, however, may reflect Ps. 37:11. Because no dominical citation formula is used as in the later section of *Didache* (9:5, e.g.), we cannot be sure which source is being used. The quotation is slightly closer to the beatitude since the article την is included in both, so this may be evidence that the Didachist is referring to the "Gospel of the Lord" and simply cites it without a formula since that seems to be his practice in this first part of the *Didache* (cf. 1:3-5).

The words that conclude the verse: "and one who trembles always at the words that you have heard," most probably are an allusion to Isa. 66:2. The qualities of meekness and humility that are to replace the "fenced" behavior forbidden in 3:1-6 must be indicated by a humble attitude toward the one who speaks the word, anticipating the clear command in 4:1. Here is a reflection of the advice in *James* 1:21: "Therefore put away all filthiness and rampant wickedness and receive with meekness the implanted word, which is able to save your souls." This is not the only parallel with *James* that has been noticed by commentators.[89]

The positive advice in this paragraph culminates in the dramatic affirmation of God's good providential ways in 3:10: "You will accept (προσδέχομαι) the experiences that happen to you as good things, knowing that nothing happens apart from God." One thinks of the Pauline affirmation in *Rom.* 8:28, but since the Didachist nowhere clearly refers to Pauline statements in any positive way, it is best to see this as echoing such passages as *Sirach* 2:4: "Accept (δέχομαι) whatever befalls you, and in times of humiliation be patient."

Five Congregational Precepts (4:1-4)

Much of the teaching up to this point for the convert from paganism has been of an individual focus – the shedding of the convert's old life and the putting on of new attitudes and behavior patterns. But the convert is joining a family in this new life—a family with brother and sisters and familial love—and also a family with potential quarrels and strife. So the life of the new believer in the body is stressed over the first few verses of chapter four.

First, his attitude toward the teacher of the word of God should be one of attention and respect (4:1). Taking the book as a whole, this probably has most immediate reference to the "overseers" (or "bishops") who have the spiritual oversight of individual congregations (15:1). Milavec views this teacher as the personal mentor of the new convert who takes him through the program described in chapters 1-5. While this is possible, in my opinion Milavec has not made a case for this individualism in training. The very next verse stresses the role of the saints as a group that provides the words on which he is to find rest and support. I believe it is best to see a combination of a teacher/overseer plus the congregation who all participate in his training. This seems more like the situation that prevailed before formal catechetical schools under the oversight of a bishop trained new converts (late second century). Milavec's view imports a bit too much of the modern mentoring under a spiritual director into the first century scene. While that may be a good idea for training young believers, it is reading too much into the text to see it here.

With his characteristic realism, the Didachist then reminds the young believer that all may not be sweetness and light in his new family. The Jerusalem manuscript states that "You will not desire (ποθήσεις) division." Many commentators suggest an emendation here as: "You will not cause (ποιήσεις) division" – the difference is only one letter. And the difference does not alter the tone of the command that much. Rather than a "division-maker," he is to be a "peace-maker" (4:3), again echoing a beatitude (Matt. 5:9). While this may appear to be a big responsibility for a novice, the command is not that he should serve on an ecclesiastical court, but simply as a brother that contributes to the unity, not to the fracturing of his new family. I personally have seen the effects that a new believer has had on the unity of the sometimes jaded older members of a congregation who ought to know better. The simplicity and love of new believers can be an example to us all.

Three Household Rules (4:9-11)

After dealing with the sharing of resources (4:5-8), the Didachist sets forth three household rules—a simple discussion of the *Haustafel*, or household code that appears often in the NT (Eph. 5:22-6:9; Col. 3:18-4:1; 1 Peter 2:18-3:7; 1 Tim. 2:8-15; Titus 2:1-10).[90] Taken together, the rules imply that there were at least some adult converts who had children and slaves. Milavec has a good summary of this passage and I cite it at length.

> In the case of children, they were trained from their earliest years "in the fear of God" (4:9). The *Didache* does not give nay guidelines as to when and how such children were to be introduced into the community. No provisions, for example, are made for infant baptisms. . . . Since the choice (to join) the community was an adult decision prompted by the Spirit (4:10b), parents were expected to train their underage children in appropriate ways until such time as they came forward, in early adulthood, and asked for admittance. In any case, parents were not to withdraw their guiding and protecting hand from their children.[91]

This passage also provides evidence of the significant social leveling that membership in the Christian family entailed. Here we see both masters and slaves who still maintain that relationship but in an entirely new and different context than was possible in society at large. And it was the Spirit's work that made this possible (4:10) by preparing both master and slave for their roles in the assembly. This is the first reference to the divine Spirit in the book, but not the last. "Holy Spirit" appears in the baptismal formula of 7:1 and 11:7-12 mentions a prophet speaking in the Spirit. The theology implied in these and other such statements of the book will be examined further in chapter nine.

Solemn Final Admonitions (4:12-14)

The new believer is told to hate the things that are not pleasing to the Lord (4:12). This prepares the reader for a list of those very things in the "Way of Death" in chapter 5. The instruction that has been given is to be carefully guarded and should neither be added to nor detracted from (4:13). This echoes Torah commands such as Deut. 4:2 and 12:32 and points out how serious this "Way of Life" was to be viewed in the community.

The final admonition points to the future when the trained convert will assume his full role as a baptized member of the church. "In church (ἐκκλησία) you will confess your wrongdoings, and you will not go to your place of prayer with an evil conscience" (4:14). The details of the weekly Eucharist have not yet been given (14:1-3). It will be in the context of that service where this admonition will find its specific focus. For the time being, however, we should know that a guilty conscience is not consistent with participation in his public "place of prayer" (προσεύχην—see its use in Acts 16:16).

Summary of the Way of Life

As has been mentioned, chapter 5 consists of a litany of at least forty attitudes and actions that comprise the "Way of Death." We will not say much about these morbid practices presented in a stark list marked by asyndeton (no conjunctions). This least attractive of the sections in the *Didache* always brings to my mind the complaints of students as we translate this chapter. They hate it because they have to look up so many unfamiliar words! I am sure the Didachist would want us to hate the sinful practices more than we hate the unfamiliar Greek lexemes!

Didache 1-5 is devoted to a teaching program that served in the church as a catechetical manual at least through the fourth century and maybe beyond. With the influx of converts from paganism in that century it must have served other catechetical schools as well as it did in Alexandria. Its contents were not to be changed or watered down (4:13, also 6:1 and 11:2). Some of the matters may have been more relevant to its original Jewish Christian concerns—for example, the next chapter. But the training program as a whole seems to have served a vital purpose as pre-baptismal catechesis for pagan converts to this newer form of Jewish faith.

Chapter Seven

The Sacraments of the *Didache*

As we move from the presentation of the "Two Ways" (1-5) to the section of the *Didache* that deals with subjects related to the life of the believer within the church (6-16), I remind my reader that we move into a section that has clear literary markers for both its beginning and ending. Furthermore, within this section are clear indications as to how it is structured by its author to present its material as a unified discourse.

First, there is an inclusio of sorts in the repetition of the statement that believers can be "perfect" in 6:2 and 16:2. Unless this is just a coincidence, the repetition indicates that bearing "the yoke of the Lord" in 6:2 is related to the charge in 16:2 to gather together frequently and find what is "appropriate for your souls." This correlation is important to note when we attempt a brief explanation for the perplexing transition of chapter six which seems to intrude between the two main sections of the *Didache*. Second, we note again the intention of the discourse marker περι δε at 6:3; 7:1; 9:1 and 11:3. Each time the marker introduces a new subject that the Didachist will discuss (food, baptism, eucharist, and apostle/prophets). Earlier we mentioned how this phrase can be seen in the Pauline correspondence when he addresses subjects in 1 Corinthians and 1 Thessalonians that have been raised by those congregations.

Over the next couple of chapters we will examine what the Didachist has to say about those four subjects under the chapter titles, "The Sacraments of the Didache" and "The Ministers of the Didache." I am only too aware that many authors have written much about these chapters and that I can only survey their ideas and offer my own perspective on them. Hopefully, these next two chapters may also prove most helpful for those who look to this early Christian document for some guidance about "doing church" today.

The Path, the Yoke, and Food (6:1-3)

It is necessary to comment on this "transitional" section before we look at the practical matters of baptism and the eucharist. The Didachist's comment and warning in 6:1 provides a conclusion to the "Two Ways" material that precedes it. "See to it that no one leads you astray from this way of teaching (δι δαχῆς), since he is teaching you apart from God." Thus the "Two Ways" section concludes with its own inclusio, since it opens with a reference to the "teaching" in 1:1.

Many writers have noticed that the words of 6:2 seem to be abruptly introduced along with the first occurrence of the περι δὲ in 6:3.

> 6:2 For, on the one hand, if you are able to bear
>   the whole yoke of the Lord, you will be perfect;
>   but if, on the other hand, you are not able,
>   that which you are able, do this.

> 6:3 And concerning (peri de.) food,
>   [1] bear that which you are able,
>   [2] but from the food sacrificed to idols,
>   especially keep away
>   for it is [related to] the worship of dead gods.

A number of recent studies have stressed the point that the passage beginning with 6:2 is neither in the Latin *Doctrina Apostolorum* nor in the parallel section in *Barnabas*. They feel that this is because the Greek "Two Ways" source used by the Didachist ended at 6:1.[92] These writers have also explained the attitude of this passage in strong counterpoint with Paul and also with the even more conservative "Jewish" position of James. One scholar even speaks of "Paul's Jewish Christian Opponents in the Didache."[93] We cannot here interact with the details of these views. Only one point will be made and an alternative view offered.

It is assumed by most writers that the necessary-to-be-borne "yoke of the Lord" in 6:2 refers to the "yoke of the Torah." This interpretation is usually set against or compared with the "Jerusalem Decree" in Acts 15. Cetainly there are some important verbal parallels with the statement by Peter in Acts 15:10, "Now, therefore, why are you putting God to the test by placing a yoke (ζυγὸν) on the neck of the disciples that neither our fathers nor we have been able to bear (βαστάσαι)?" Peter refers to the yoke of Torah. There are two other uses of the word "yoke" in the NT which should also be considered. The first is the strong statement by Paul in Gal. 6:1, "For freedom Christ has set us free; stand firm therefore, and do not submit again to a yoke (ζυγῷ) of slavery." Paul is obviously referring again to the yoke of Torah. The other use of the word is by Jesus in Matt. 11:29, 30, "Take my yoke (ζυγόν) upon you, and learn from me, for I am gentle and lowly in heart, and you will find rest for your souls. For my yoke (ζυγός) is easy, and my burden is light."

The suggestion here is that the yoke is not that of the Jewish Torah but, as the verse states, it is the yoke of "the Lord." Since the "Lord" elsewhere in *Di-*

dache refers to Jesus (see "Gospel of our Lord" in 15:4), it seems to be forced to make this a reference to the Torah, as it is in Acts and Galatians. Furthermore, the Didachist had used phrase "you will be perfect" (ἔσῃ τέλειος) at the beginning of his "evangelical" section in 1:4. Thus, he recalls once again the commands of the Lord that he quoted in 1:3b-2:1. They are for him "the yoke of the Lord" and so make up the new Torah of Jesus. Yes, he recognizes the serious nature of the Lord's commandments, and those who are not able to obey all these commands fully should at least do what they can. *Didache* scholars who have contributed significant commentaries on the book also have acknowleged this view as the preferred one.[94] When this view of the "yoke" is recognized, it frees the interpreter from having to align this statement with those of James, Peter and Paul and then posit the degree of agreement or disagreement with them. While such a discussion is valid, caution should be used in employing 6:2 as a strong peiece of evidence in that discussion.

In 6:3 the Didachist introduces his next subject, food, and offers some very succinct teaching. The young believers should "bear that which you are able, but from the food sacrificed to idols, especially keep away for it is [related to] the worship of dead gods." While all the obligations of the Torah are not required, there is concern about the food laws, even though the commands of the Torah that relate exclusively to the Jewish people are not expected to be obeyed. The Didachist's advice is nuanced and also reveals a pastoral sensitivity. The eating of meat sacrificed to idols, on the other hand, is absolutely forbidden. As for the other food laws, individuals may observe them to the extent possible for each one. Converts from Gentile backgrounds may find some of the dietary laws extremely difficult to obey. On the other hand, concern for Jewish sensitivities in this regard should motivate a total abstinence from idolatry—something in their pagan background that simply can't be countenanced in their new lives. While Paul may have nuanced this further to keep from binding the conscience, their advice, in my opinion, is still moving in the same trajectory.

Baptism (7:1-4)

Sad to say, most laymen and many ministers show little knowledge of the *Didache*. If there is one thing that they do know about this book, it is that "it teaches that you can baptize any way that you want." On the one hand, Baptists like its emphasis on immersion, but do not like its permission of pouring if you lack adequate water. On the other hand, Presbyterians like its flexibility about the mode of baptism, but do not like its preference for immersion. And neither Baptists nor Presbyterians are too excited about that preference for cold and flowing water! Hopefully, there is some way to approach chapter seven without this baggage of denominational agendas getting in the way!

For the sake of comparison, I quote the entire chapter with my translation.

7:1 And concerning baptism, baptize this way:

> After you have said all these things beforehand,
> immerse in the name of the Father

and of the Son
and of the Holy Spirit
in flowing water.

7:2 [1] but if you (sg.) do not have flowing water,
immerse in other water;
[2] and if you are not able to do so in cold,
[immerse] in warm [water];
7:3 [3] and if you should not have either,
pour out water onto the head three times
in the name of the Father
and of the Son
and of the Holy Spirit.
7:4 And prior to the baptism,
[1] let the one baptizing fast;
[2] also one being baptized
[3] and if any others are able to do so;
And order the one being baptized to fast
one or two [days] before.

Willy Rordorf has briefly summarized the main historical issues related to the chapter in an excellent article.[95] His conclusions are succinctly stated and avoid the denominational agendas mentioned above.

The text is striking less for what it says than for what it does not say. One can clearly observe that this short text does not transmit the entire formula of the baptismal rite. But only those aspects of baptism which one could not assurdly pass over in silence, if one had known them. Let us try to summarize them.
a) The renunciation of Satan is not mentioned. Moreover, one has the impression that this rite would have been included in the kind of work which sanctions the teaching of the "two ways" in Didache 1-6.
b) The consecration of the water seems to be unknown in the *Didache*.
c) There is no trace of the Pauline theology of baptism.
d) What is most striking is the absence of the laying on of hands and of any mention of the gift of the Holy Spirit at the moment of baptism. G.W.H. Lampe has shown that ths old tradition was more widespread at the beginning of Christianity than one would think at first sight. The *Didache* must be linked to that strem of the tradition, which is a sign of its archaic character.[96]

Since baptism is a subject that is so interwined with theology and history, the approach of a theologically informed church historian is helpful. Philip Schaff, an eminent church historian, was one of the earliest scholars in the English speaking world who thoroughly investigated the *Didache* after its publication. I will offer a summary of the baptismal chapter along the lines that he developed in the second edition of his thorough study of the *Didache*.[97] His ideas will be supplemented with my own personal comments at particular points where appropriate. Schaff infers the following particulars about baptism as practiced by the community of the *Didache*.

1. Baptism was to take place after a period of instruction in the Way of Life and the Way of Death. Nothing is said about infant baptism. The references to instruction and fasting indicate that the Didachist has in view only the baptism of catechumens, or adult believers. In the apostolic church and in the ante-Nicene age baptism of believing converts was the rule. In the New Testament the baptized are addressed as people who have doed and risen with Christ. Thus, in the NT baptism and conversion are almost used as synonymous terms (Acts 2:38, 41; Rom. 6:3, 4; Gal. 3:27). In an instructive lecture presented at the Oxford Apostolic Fathers conference in April, 2004, Professor David Wright asked if the Apostolic Fathers broke the silence of the New Testament about infant baptism. He concluded that they did not.[98] At the end of the second century, Tertullian mentions the practice, although he opposed it as imprudent. Within fifty years, however, Origen wrote approvingly of the practice (*To Romans*, 50, 5, 6). As a church historian and Presbyterian, Schaff did not think that such silence in the apostolic period argues against the practice. Inclusion of children in the rite was necessitated when Christianity became established and family religion with its duties and privileges thus emerged.

2. Baptism must be administered into the triune name (εἰς τὸ ὄνομα) **of the Father, and the Son, and the Holy Spirit.** This is the form prescribed by Jesus in Matt. 28:19, 20. The shorter form "into the name of Jesus" is not mentioned, but in 9:5 the requirement for partaking of the eucharist is that one must be "baptized into the name of the Lord" (εἰς ὄνομα κυρίου). This variation and freedom of expression is characteristic of NT usage as well (see the name of Jesus in Acts 8:16; 10:48; 19:5; Rom. 6:3; Gal. 3:27), and should not be viewed as evidence of different authors or redactors. The use of the singular "name" before the three persons is indicative of a Trinitarian viewpoint – before the word "trinity" was coined in the late second century.

3. The normal and most favored mode of baptism is three-fold immersion in "living water," i.e., fresh, running water in either a stream or lake, as distinct from standing water in a pool or cistern. Immersion must be intended by the imperative verb βαπτισατε, otherwise there would be no difference between the first mode and the last which is clearly pouring (ἔκχεον). The preference for a river not only derives from the Savior's baptism in the Jordan, but also was consistent with the Jewish *mikveh* practice of always being done in "living water."[99]

4. While preference is given to immersion in living water, the *Didache* allows three exceptions: (a) **Baptism by immersion "into other water"** (εἰς ἄλλο ὕδωρ), *i.e.* any other kind of cold water in pools or cisterns. (b) **Baptism by immersion in warm water** (in houses), when the health of the candidate or the inclemency of the climate or season may require it. (c) **Threefold aspersion of the head, where neither running nor standing, nor cold nor warm water is at hand in sufficient quantity for total immersion.** The aspersion of the head was the nearest substitute for total immersion, since the head is the chief part of man. There can be no baptism without baptizing the head; but there *may be* valid baptism without baptizing the rest of the body.

Here we have the oldest extant testimony for the validity of baptism by pouring or aspersion. The reason given is not the health of the one baptized (clinical baptism). The *Didache* puts it simply on the ground of scarcity of water, so that healthy persons might likewise be baptized (*e.g.* if converted in a desert, or on a mountain, or in a prison, or in a catacomb.) We have, therefore, a right to infer that at the end of the first century there was no rigid uniformity in regard to the *mode* of baptism and no scruple about the validity of the aspersion or pouring, provided only the head was baptized into the triune name with the intention of baptizing.

Thus explained, the directions of the *Didache* are perfectly clear and consistent with all the other information we have on baptism in the ante-Nicene age. Trine immersion into the triune name was the rule, as it is to this day in all the Oriental churches. Triune aspersion or pouring was the exception. The new thing which we learn is this: that in the post-Apostolic age a degree of freedom prevailed on the mode of baptism, which was afterwards somewhat restricted. Schaff concludes, "From this fact we may reason, (*a fortiori*) that the same freedom existed already in the apostolic age. It cannot be supposed that the Twelve Apostles were less liberal than the writer of the *Didache*, who wrote as it were in their name."[100]

It is astonishing how this ancient testimony has been twisted and turned by certain writers in their own party interest. Some exclusive immersionists, in order to get rid of the exception, have even declared the *Didache* a literary forgery, or subject to later editing by compromising proto-Presbyterians. Some zealous advocates of sprinkling as the supposed original and Scriptural mode have turned the exception into the rule, and substituted an imaginary difference between pouring in running water and pouring on dry ground for the real difference between immersion and pouring water on the head.

5. Baptism is to be preceded by fasting on the part of both the catechumen and the baptizer and some others who may join. The former is required to fast one or two days. There is no such prescription in the New Testament. In the case of Christ fasting *followed* his Baptism (Matt 4:2). The three thousand Pentecostal converts seem to have been baptized on the day of their conversion (Acts 2:38-40). Fasting is likewise mentioned as customary in connection with Baptism by Justin Martyr and Tertullian, but not so definitely as the *Didache*. The fasting of the baptizer probably soon went out of use.

6. Baptism is not represented as a clerical function, but the directions are addressed to all members of the congregation. In the corresponding direction of the *Apostolic Constitutions* the bishop or presbyter is addressed, and Ignatius restricts the right to baptize to the bishop, or at all events requires his permission or presence. Justin Martyr mentions no particular person as the approved officiant. Tertullian, in his Montanist opposition to a special priesthood, expressly gives the right even to laymen, when bishops, priests, or deacons are not at hand.[101]

7. No mention is made of exorcism, which preceded the act of Baptism, nor of the application of oil, salt, or other material, which accompanied it as early as the second and third centuries. The silence is conclusive, not indeed against the use of these additions, but against their importance in the estimation of the writer and his age. As has been observed so often in these matters, this is another indication of the early date of the *Didache*.

Fasting and Prayer (8:1-3)

The mention of fasting accompanying baptism leads the Didachist into a brief discussion of fasting and how it is *not* to be done like the "hypocrites" (8:1). Although other views have been maintained about the identity of these "hypocrites," it still seems best to see the influence of the Matthean "Gospel of the Lord" and interpret them as Pharisaic Jews who were in the area of the *Didache* community.[102] The verbal similarities to canonical Matthew 6 (fasting, prayer, Lord's Prayer, hypocrites) in 7:5-8:2 are quite striking, although the two works discuss the subjects in a different order and context. We discussed the textual features of the *Didache*'s "Lord's Prayer" in chapter six.

The Eucharist (9:1-10:7; 14:1-3)

The third appearance of the marker περὶ δὲ in 9:1 introduces the subject of the "eucharist" (εὐχαριστία) or "thanksgiving meal." This discussion continues through chapter ten and is picked up again, although in a different way, in chapter fourteen. Johannes Betz has succinctly summarized the challenge facing the interpreter of these chapters.

> The famous Meal Prayers of chapters 9 and 10 are also among the most diffi-
> cult and contested problems of *Didache* research. Their main content consists
> of prayers which are certainly older than the writing as a whole. That they al-
> ready originated early and derive from the pre-*Didache* Aramaic community is
> indicated by their formal and material proximity to Jewish formulae (*Berakot*),
> from the Aramaic cries of *Hosanna* and *Maranatha*, from the baptism into the
> Lord (Jesus) attested here, from the ancient *Pais*-Christology, as generally form
> their Jewish-Christian theology. The whole stands under the title "eucharist." In
> any case, what exactly is meant by this is, to this day, a contested question and
> a problem which continues to be posed.[103]

As is often the case, Willy Rordorf has handled the challenge of this material ably and offers an excellent synthesis of the three chapters.[104] I acknowledge his influence on my own approach to these chapters.

These chapters represent a transitional link between the Jewish tradition represented in the table blessings (the *Birkat Hamazon*) and the eucharistic liturgies preserved in the later formularies for the Christian Mass. In these primitive liturgies we very much observe prayers in their Jewish cradle.[105] The Jewish prayers, however, are Christianized in their adaptation for the *Didache* congregations. We set out an analytical translation of the chapters.

10:1   And after being filled, give thanks in this way:

10:2   We give you thanks, holy Father,
        For your holy name,
        Which you have caused to dwell in our hearts,
        And for the knowledge and faith and immortality
        Which you revealed to us through your servant Jesus.
            To you is the glory forever.

10:3   You, almighty Master,
        Created all things for the sake of your name,
        Both food and drink you have given to people for enjoyment
            in order that they might give thanks.
        But to us you have graciously bestowed spiritual food and
            drink and eternal life through your servant.

10:4   Before all things, we give you thanks because you are powerful.
            To you is the glory forever.
10:5   Remember, Lord, your church,
        to save her from every evil,
        and to perfect her in your love
        and to gather her together from the four winds,
        the saints into your kingdom which you have prepared for her.
            Because yours is the power and the glory forever.
10:6   [A] May grace come and may this world pass away!
        [B] Hosanna to the God of David! (cf. Matt. 21:9)
        [C] If anyone is holy, let him come!
            If anyone is not, let him repent!
        [D] Come Lord [maranatha]! Amen!

10:7   But allow the prophets to "give thanks" as much as they wish.

The main question facing the interpreter is why there are two separate sections describing the "eucharist." I consider the approach that considers such "repetition" as evidence of a later clumsy redactor as being too facile, and I rather accept the integrity of the Bryennios manuscript as it is. But why are there two treatments? I accept the proposal that chapters nine and ten contain, not a eucharistic liturgy in the strict sense, but prayers spoken at table before the eucharist proper. Furthermore, the "text contains prayers originally used at table during communal meals, and that these prayers were given eucharistic overtones because the eucharist followed immediately on the communal meal."[106]

In his massive commentary, Jean Audet provides abundant evidence of how influential was the ancient Jewish tradition of thanking God.[107] In this view, held in varying ways by many authors, chapters nine and ten describe an *agape*, or ordinary breaking of bread. The prayers are blessings said at that meal, as 10:1

makes clear, "And after being filled, give thanks in this way." They form what one has called "a Christian *Birkat Hamazon* in a Passover setting."[108] This meal was then followed by the eucharist, which 10:6 introduces by offering the invitation, "If anyone is holy, let him come! If anyone is not, let him repent!" The reason for the divergence into a discussion of prophets and apostles (11-13) is due to the statement to allow the prophets to "eucharistize" as much as they wish (10:7). The divergence also thus separates the agape from the "main eucharist" in space as well as time.

In the Jewish table blessings, there was a thanksgiving for bread and wine and after the meal there was a lengthy prayer of blessing at whch foreigners, women, slaves, and children were not present. In the *Didache* prayers, this would correspond to the restriction on non-baptized persons partaking of the meal (9:5). Rordorf further cites the evidence of Hippolytus' *Apostolic Traditon*, which prohibits catechumens from partaking in the *agape*.[109]

There is similarity and there is, of course, difference between the Didache's form of the prayers and the traditional Jewish form. Christians took the Jewish blessings over the bread and wine and gave them a new meaning. The wine recalls the vine of David, the hidden meaning which has been revealed in the passion of the Messiah, the Isaianic suffering servant (παῖς). The bread is the bread that was broken—a sign of salvation and a pledge of life for all believers who eat of it. The implications of this παῖς-Christology are obscured by versions which translate this key word as "child."[110] The implications of this word for explaining the evident lack of sacrificial language in these prayers will be explored in a later chapter on the theology of the Didache.

Chapter 14 then states the following:

14:1 And on the Lord's day of the Lord,
    when you are gathered together, break bread.
      [A] And give thanks, having before confessed your failings,
        so that your sacrifice may be pure.
14:2   [B] However, let no one having a conflict with his comrade,
      come together with you until they have been reconciled,
        in order that your sacrifice may not be defiled.

14:3   For this [sacrifice] is that which was spoken by the Lord:
      "In every place and time, offer to me a pure sacrifice."
      "Because I am a great king," says the Lord,
      "and my name will be wondrous among the Gentiles."

This chapter adds the following details not mentioned in chapters 9 and 10.

1. The meeting takes place on "Lord's day of the Lord" (κατὰ κυριακὴν δὲ κυρίου). Despite this overly full expression, the reference is doubtless to a Sunday, being the new day for specifically Christian worship. It should be noted that in a book which is so Jewish in its expression and context, worship on the first day of the week and not the seventh is strongly emphasized. By the time of Igna-

tius and *"Barnabas"* the practice of Sunday worship is very obvious, although some may affirm that this was a predominantly Gentile church (*Magnesians* 9: 1, 2; *Barnabas* 15). But in a first century Jewish-Christian work, the lack of continued Sabbath observance may come as a surprise to some modern Messianic Jews who desire to maintain that practice. *Didache* 8:1 attacks "hypocrites" who fast on days two and five while urging believers to fast on days four and six. Rordorf asks, "May we suppose that in emphasizing the fact that the meeting is on Sunday, *Didache* 14, 1 is making a similar point against those who would make Saturday the preferred day of worship? We cannot say so with certainty, but the possibility is not to be excluded since other texts from the same period show that such a 'temptation' existed."[111] In addition to the *Magnesians* reference above, he refers to Gal. 4:8-11 and Col. 2:16, 17 as evidence for this temptation to continue Sabbath observance among Jewish and Gentile Christians.

2. If the Sunday meeting is the same as the one described in 9 and 10, it must also have included a communal meal. It follows that the meal was taken in the evening, since that would be when a meal is taken and work obligations would have prevented something as important as this in the daytime. Rordorf cites the famous *Letter of Pliny the Younger* where he mentions a meal of the Christians on Sunday evening.[112] I am not convinced that Sunday evening was the practice of the *Didache* believers, since in Jewish custom the evening marks the beginning of the next day and such a meal on the first day of the week (*Acts* 20:7) would be satisfied by one on Saturday evening. In any case, these chapters belong to a period when the *agape* and the eucharist had not yet been separated.

3. We see that the breaking of bread and thanksgiving (eucharist) were accompanied by a confession of sins. This same command was already given in 4:14. As we compare the two passages, it appears that 14:1 is a sort of elaborated commentary on the earlier passage. The confession here is also communal (note the plural εὐχαριστήσατε and προσεξομολογησάμενοι) while the confession in 4:14 is individual (the singular ἐξομολογήσῃ). The individual catechumen is taught to confess his sins, but he joins with the community later as he confesses at the eucharist. Furthermore, 14:2 states that those sins can include an unreconciled dispute between spiritual "comrades." This should remind the reader of Matt. 5:23, 24, which refers to the Temple offering when Jesus uttered them. His words, however, were adapted to the new situation of Christian worship.

4. Rordorf states that he "would not attach much importance to the use of the word "sacrifice."[113] I agree. It is simply wrong to read the practice of later Christian sacramental practices into this early Jewish context. Clearly these texts, in appealing to Mal. 1:11, 14, are contrasting this new type of sacrifice with the bloody sacrifices of the Old Covenant. As was mentioned in a previous chapter, this approach would be in agreement with the NT texts which speak of the Christian sacrifices being spiritual and consisting of praise and thanksgiving. To utilize them as being some sort of preliminary teaching about the sacrifice of the mass is grossly anachronistic.

Finally, like its description in the NT, the eucharist of the Didache has an eschatological focus as well. Consider the emphasis of 9:4, "Just as this broken bread was scattered over the mountains, and was gathered together and became one, in this way, may your church be gathered together from the ends of the earth into your kingdom." A local community, gathered around what is but a small fragment, recognizes that it is part of a larger loaf, or body to change the metaphor, that will be gathered into the future kingdom.

Chapter Eight

The Ministers of the *Didache*

Overseers and Deacons (15)

A unique picture of the church emerges from the *Didache*. We are given an invaluable glimpse of a community that is making or has just made the transition from a regime of prophets and teachers to one of overseers and deacons (15:1, 2). The author has to reassure his readers that the order of the eucharist celebrated by these new officials is just as good as that of the prophets and teachers. But it is still regarded as normal and desirable that each local church should have its prophet and teacher. Any authentic prophet or teacher who is willing to stay should be welcomed and supported by the church, "for they are your high priests" (13:1-3).

But we have started at the end, and perhaps it would be best to retrace the steps that brought the Didachist to this point. It will also be necessary to compare what we read in the *Didache* with some statements from the NT and also from the *Shepherd of Hermas* so we may get a better picture of the "ministers" who served the churches during this formative period.[114]

Teachers (11-13)

One reason why prophets and teachers are so welcome in the churches at this period of time is that this is a church that has not yet developed more than the most basic doctrines about Christian belief and practice. While we shall see in a later chapter that while there exists a theological substructure underlying the *Didache*, it is just that—a structure that lies beneath the many admonitions, mostly out of the reader's view. Even with that recognition, all must agree that we are reading about churches that were still in their infancy in the area of a developed theology. Therefore, anyone who can "add to its righteousness and knowledge of the Lord is to be received 'as the Lord' " (11:2).

This dependence on "charismatic leaders," however, posed several problems. First of all, there was the great difficulty, widely encountered in the early Christian centuries, when the hospitality which Christians were expected to practice towards visitors could easily be exploited. This was so well known that the pagan writer, Lucian, was able to make a story of it.[115] The Didachist, therefore, gives some rules to help the community to deal with visitors. "Everyone who comes in the name of the Lord is to be welcomed," but after the initial welcome, the church should adopt a more stringent attitude. A traveler is to be helped as much as possible, but he must not stay for more than three days at the most. If he wants to remain, he must earn his keep by doing some work. The Didachist leaves it to the good sense of the community to decide what to do with someone who has no crafts or skills, but, in any case, no Christian is to be allowed to live in idleness. Any visitor who refuses to abide by these terms is to be shunned as a "Christ-peddler" (χριστέμπορος). This word was probably coined by the Didachist since it is the first known reference to it in Greek literature.[116] One should not miss the vivid contrast that the author has deftly made by using this word immediately after his only use of the word "Christian" in the previous verse. There the word describes a worthy vistor who settles down in the community (12:1-5), unlike the fraud who is a "Christ-peddler."

Genuine prophets and teachers, on the other hand, deserve to be supported without having to do any other work. They should be given the first fruits of all the produce and income of the community (13:1-7). But how are genuine teachers to be recognized? The primary criterion is a doctrinal one. Referring back to the ethical and liturgical instructions which occupy the first ten chapters of the Didache, the author says, "Therefore, whoever teaches you all these things said previously, receive him. If, on the other hand, the one teaching, if he has been turned, and should teach another doctrine for the destroying [of those things], do not listen to him" (11:1, 2a). Any teaching which undermines the "apostolic tradition" which our compiler has presented to us is automatically regarded as disqualifying the would-be teacher. As was mentioned at the beginning of the chapter, this same passage states that new teaching, by contrast, which proposes some development in the understanding of Christian faith and practice, is acceptable, provided it is compatible with what has already been received. One wonders if the Didachist himself is one of those teachers. This is a "teaching" (διδαχη), and teaching requires a teacher (διδάσκαλος).

Since we have referred to the Didachist a number of times anonymously, it is appropriate at this point to raise the question of his identity. Obviously, he did not intend to tell us his name. No patristic reference to the *Didache* ever assigns an author but simply mentions the "apostles" in connection with its title. While I hesitate in trembling to be dogmatic, I am reminded of some authors today who confidently will attribute the letter "To the Hebrews" to Paul or to Apollos or even to Priscilla! If they can do that with an anonymous book, perhaps I will be allowed to express at least an opinion and leave it at that.

I refer to one of the greatest writers on the book—the church historian, Philip Schaff. Schaff summarized the evidence as follows.[117] The author was undoubtedly a Jewish Christian who emphasized the legal and moral in Christianity. He showed no influence from Paul. It could be said he was ante-Pauline, but not anti-Pauline. Schaff makes the telling point that if the Didachist was opposed to Paul, the book would never have been recommended by Athanasius and other fathers for catechetical instruction.[118] And yet, his style and phraseology are Hebraic. Except for his criticism of the "hypocrites" (the Pharisees), he abstains from polemics against the Jewish people and their religion, and this differs from the so-called *Letter of Barnabas*. While he commends the morality of the Torah, he knows the love, meekness and generosity of the Gospel. And yet, his message was primarily for the Gentiles and he placed no other yoke on them but that of the "Lord." While concluding that his identity will probably never be known, Schaff refers approvingly to the opinion of Canon Spence that the best conjecture is that the author was Simeon of Jerusalem, son of Cleopas, nephew of Joseph and cousin of the Lord. According to Hegessipus and Eusebius, Simeon succeeded James the Lord's brother as leader of the Jerusalem congregation. He also led that church during its removal to Pella beyond the Jordan, where that entirely Jewish church began to grow in non-Jewish soil (the Decapolis) for the first time. He fits the character of the writing and is in the time period of the *Didache*'s writing—from the mid-60's. His relocation with the Jerusalem congregation to Pella fits its rural setting in an area that is known for its Jewish-Christian congregations in Gentile areas – the trans-Jordan region as part of Southern Syria, near Damascus and within the orbit of Antiochene influence. It was first said by Origen about the work, "To the Hebrews" that only God knows its author for sure. Even Origen, however, conjectured that the book's author was Paul. So the same appeal must also be made to divine knowledge about the authorship of *Didache*. But that doesn't mean that we are forbidden to conjecture, like Origen did, about who might have been its author.

Whoever the teacher was who authored the Didache, he was familiar not only with the role of plain teachers, he was aware of two special kinds of itinerant teachers. These two called for more specific treatment, though they were all naturally still subject to the basic doctrinal criterion. These were apostles and prophets.

Apostles (11)

The fourth appearance of the discourse marker περι δε is in 11:3: "And concerning (περι δε) the apostles and prophets in accord with the decree of the gospel, act thus." Thus chapters 11-14 are primarily concened with these two "ministers"- the apostles and the prophets. While we cannot prove the Didachist's dependence on Paul, one is reminded of the similarity between the Didachist and the Pauline statements that list the "ministers" who were gifts to the church. "And God has appointed in the church first apostles, second prophets, third teachers" (1 Cor. 12:28a). "And he gave the apostles, the prophets, the evangelists, the pastors and teachers" (Eph. 4:11). How were they different and how were they similar?

"Apostles" were expected to conform to a rather stricter version of the rules governing all Christian travelers that we have mentioned above. They were allowed to stay for only one day, or two if necessary. If they stayed for a third day, that was enough to reveal them as "false prophets." At their departure they were to be given only enough bread to last them until their next destination. If they asked for money, once again they were exposed as phony (11:4-6).

These "apostles" are evidently not to be identified with the Twelve. They are rather the successors of the seventy two itinerant preachers sent out by Jesus (cf. Luke 10:1-11). They are also an important link in the development of the itinerant monasticism characteristic of the Syrian church. The hardening of itinerancy into a rule making it compulsory to move on nearly every day was presumably the result of a combination of apostolic urgency and the need to protect the hosts of the wandering preachers from having their hospitality unfairly exploited or overburdened.[119]

What precisely was the role of these apostles is not clear. No liturgical office is ascribed to them. It is only prophets and teachers who are described in 15:1: "they likewise conduct among you the ministry" (λειτουργοῦσι καὶ αὐτοὶ τὴν λειτουργίαν). Nor is there any suggestion that the content of their teaching differed from that of other teachers. The fact of their constant wandering might imply that their task was to provide basic instruction in the Christian faith, which could then be elaborated by more settled teachers. Against this interpretation, however, is the initial statement which welcomes teachers of any kind that can add to the church's knowledge and righteousness of the Lord (11:2). Furthermore, teachers other than apostles seemed not to settle down any more than apostles do (13:1, 2). It is unlikely that there is any rigorous distinction between apostles and other teachers; any more than there is between today's pastoral clergy and visiting preachers. The essential distinction was that **apostles were not allowed to settle down**, whereas other teachers were free to stay or to move on as they pleased or in response to the need of the churches.

Prophets in Spirit (11)

"Prophets" were distinguished from other teachers in that they "spoke in spirit." Although it is not clear exactly what speaking in spirit means, it was evidently a phenomenon that could be recognized at once. Presumably the Didachist is referring to the same phenomenon that Paul referred to in 1 Cor. 12:3, and, like Paul, it shows an awareness that the spirit spoken of is not the "Holy Spirit." Notice the initially odd statement, "Not everyone who speaks in spirit is a prophet" (11:8). We may presume that, however it was manifested, speaking in spirit involved making utterances purporting to come from God and so claiming the authority of divine revelation. It was therefore crucial to have some criteria by which to judge whether the revelation was genuine or not, particularly in a church as ill-equipped in doctrine like that of the *Didache*. Paul proposes a very simple test. If someone speaking in spirit was able to say, "Jesus is Lord," the inspiration comes from the Holy Spirit. If instead the person curses Jesus, then another spirit is at work. Since speaking in spirit is not something that operates beyond the control of the speaker (1 Cor. 14:32), the Pauline test can presumably be applied by requiring the speaker to confess "Jesus is Lord" and then to see what happens. Paul had no qualms about subjecting both the behavior and the words of the prophets to the critical judgment of the church (1 Cor. 14:29-

33). The Didachist does not share his confidence. He knows that sins against the Holy Sprit cannot be forgiven, and he identifies this kind of sin with presuming to question or discriminate between prophetic utterances (11:7). No doubt a prophet who infringed on the basic doctrinal principles governing all kinds of teachers would thereby be disqualified. The Didachist himself in fact notes other things which someone speaking in spirit might say, which would reveal him to be a false prophet. In this context appears the strange dscription in 11:9, "And every prophet ordering a table in the Spirit will not eat from it, and if he does, he is a false prophet." Many interpreters view the "table" here as the eucharistic table, in the sense of "convening a eucharistic assembly."[120] It is best, however, to view this table (τραπέζα) as a metonymy for a meal, as it is so used in *Acts* 6:2; 16:34, and *Diognetus* 5:7.[121] If a prophet claims to be in the spirit when he requests food, he should indicate that the request finds its origin in the spirit and demonstrate that fact by not partaking of the meal himself.

That this "table" is a common and not a liturgical one also seems more consistent with the following restriction in 11:12, "If anyone says, 'Give me money' or anything else, do not listen to him." But, for the Didachist, the supreme test is how the prophet behaves. What has to be discovered is whether one who claims to speak in spirit is a genuine prophet or not. It is only the words of genuine prophets that cannot be criticized without sinning against the Holy Spirit. Although it may sometimes be possible to convict a false prophet on the basis of what he says, what is looked for primarily is that the prophet should have "the manners of the Lord" and that he should practice what he preaches. If he asks for money or other gifts, it must be for the benefit of the poor. Thus, as was previously noted, if he orders a meal "in spirit," it must be for others, and he must not eat it himself (11:7-12).

A speaker in spirit who passes the test and is recognized as a "true, tested prophet" (11:10) is exempt from critical assessment. His words must be accepted simply as coming from God. In the church of the Didache there can be no question of revelation being already closed or completed. Further revelation was both needed and expected. And if the prophet did strange things, like the prophets of the Old Testament, it was for God to judge him, provided that he did not try to incite his hearers to behave likewise. This is probably the best approach to handling that controversial description in 11:11: "And every prophet who has been put to the test and is genuine, and who acts for the earthly mystery of the church, but not teaching to do what he himself does, he shall not be judged by you; for he has his judgment from God, for also the ancient prophets so acted."

Prophets in the Apostolic Fathers

There are 62 references to the words "prophet" or "prophets" in the Apostolic Fathers. *Clement, Ignatius, Barnabas, Diognetus,* and *Papias* use the word 28 times to designate only the Old Testament prophets. Apart from the *Didache*, only the *Shepherd of Hermas* uses the word (13 times) to apply to the "New Testament prophets" in his own day. He also uses the word "prophetic" once, again of the prophets during his time (43:1-16). *Didache* uses the word in singular and plural 21 times. Therefore, only *Didache* and *Hermas* speak of prophets during their times. The only other author who may use the word in a similar fashion is the author of the *Martyrdom of Polycarp*, who speaks of the martyr twice as "prophetic." This commonality of discussion between the two books raises the question of the possible influence of one on the other. While there are not many scholars who would affirm it, the more elaborate discussion in *Hermas* indicates, in my opinion, that he is the most probable one to be influenced by the *Didache*, and not vice-versa. An additional issue is that his description of church leaders as "presbyters" without any reference to monepiscopacy in *Hermas* may point to a first century date of that book, which is often assigned to the mid-second century.

In *Hermas* 43 there is a similar discussion to that in *Didache* 11-13. There it is emphasized also that one can know a true prophet by his life. As in the *Didache*, prophets are to be tested on the basis of their lives (43.7), but Hermas also indicates a simple criterion by which the true can be distinguished from the false on the basis of their respective ways of operating. The false prophet identifies himself as "bearing the Spirit" (43.16) and positively attracts customers from whom he expects payment (43.12). He functions just like a pagan oracle, answering people's questions but otherwise having nothing to say (43. 2, 6). His services are strictly private and if he is in the assembly of the righteous who are full of faith and are praying to God, he finds himself struck dumb (43. 13-14). His clients are typically people full of doubts and dilemmas, staggering from one crisis to the next, needing authoritative guidance about what they are to do (43. 2, 4). The false prophet assures them with a mixture of truth and falsehood, but the spirit at work in him comes from the devil (43.3), and is earthly, powerless and foolish (43.11) deserving of no confidence whatsoever (43.17).

A true prophet, by contrast, never answers questions and never operates in private. In the Christian assembly, when prayer is made, the "angel of the prophetic spirit" fills him, and being filled with the Holy Spirit, he speaks as "the Lord wills" (43.9). The Spirit at work in him is from God and is therefore powerful and should be trusted (43.17). He would be quite incapable of accepting any remuneration for his services (43.12).

One of the moral qualities looked for in a true prophet is that "he makes himself needier than anyone" (43.8). At first sight, this suggests an ascetic renunciation of possessions. However, a very similar expression appears in a list of qualities in connection with which no one should practice self control. So it is most unlikely that *Hermas*, who is elsewhere so indulgent toward rich Christians, is recommending voluntary poverty to everyone. Such an interpretation would make sense of some of the other good things in the list which could only be practiced by people with money (38.10). So what *Hermas* is calling for in the attitude of the true prophet is proper for all Christians to adopt – one of radical humility and dependence.

In conclusion, while there are a number of parallels with *Didache*, the *Hermas* discussion of prophets is more nuanced and contains more alternative possibilities and alternatives than the simpler situation presented in *Didache*.

Overseers and Deacons Again (15)

In our discussion of the ministers of the *Didache*, we must now return to where we began the chapter. Much has been written about the commands issued in 15:1: "Appoint, then, for yourselves, overseers and deacons worthy of the Lord, gentle men and not money lovers and truthful and tested; for they likewise conduct among you the ministry of the prophets and teachers." I have adopted the translation "overseers" rather than the traditional "bishops" for the Greek word οἰκονομοὶ. The word "bishop" bears too much the idea of the later monarchical bishop and is a bit anachronistic for the first century church.

Most scholars believe that the early Jewish-Christian churches followed the organizational pattern of the Jewish synagogue. Indeed the word "synagogue" is used once in the NT for the place of Jewish Christian worship (James 2:2). If this be the case, it should be noted that one group of synagogue leaders were the elders (πρεσβύτεροι). Indeed that title seems to be synonymous and interchangeable with the οἰκόνομοι in passages that discuss the leaders of early churches in the New Testament (*1 Tim.* 3:1, 2; 5:19; *Titus* 1:5, 7; *Acts* 20:17, 28; *1 Peter* 5:1). These same two titles in 15:1 are used by Paul in the greeting to the church in Philippi (*Phil.* 1:1).

One may inquire why the Didachist chose the word "overseer" instead of "elder." As a matter of fact, the last word does not even appear in his book. This choice was probably due to the fact that congregations with a significant Gentile membership were in view. The word οἰκόνομοι would have a more familiar ring to Gentile readers in describing what basically was the function of this person (oversight) rather than referring to the maturity of the person in view (elder).

Didache 15:1, 2 is clear on one matter. These overseers and deacons did not derive their authority from the apostles and prophets, but through the medium of the local churches themselves. It was the churches that were to appoint for themselves these leaders. The chapter continues that these leaders were to be worthy of the Lord, meek and unselfish, truthful and of good report and were to be honored like the prophets and teachers (15:1, 2). Many of these character traits are quite similar to the similar lists in 1 Tim. 3 and Titus 1.

This is all we learn of the two classes of permanent congregational officers. We assume that the overseers were the regular teachers who had spiritual oversight of the flock. This is based on the fact that the only discernible difference for the overseer from the deacon in *1 Tim.* 3 is that the overseer must be "able to teach" (*1 Tim.* 3:2). The deacons were the helpers who attend to the tempral needs of the congregation, especially the care of the poor and the sick. While we cannot be dogmatic beyond those assumptions, the definite impression is that this book is being written during the passing of a wandering charismatic leadership and the permanent arrival of a local and settled leadership. This is not meant it imply that the overseers and deacons were some new means of leading the flock. It is just that soon they would be the sole leaders on the local scene and the congregations need to recognize the importance of their permanent leadership roles. In the earlier section of the "two ways," the catechumen was exhorted to give close attention to the one who teaches the word of God and to honor him as he would the Lord (4:1). Now this same command is re-issued because the overseers and deacons are their "honored ones" (15:2).

In later years, the deaconate became a steppingstone to the presbyterate, or priesthood. There is no hint of that situation here—another indiocation of the archaic character of the book. Thus, no evidence can be found here.of a three-fold ministry (bishop/presbyter/deacon) that began to emerge in the second century. *The Apostolic Constitutions*, which takes over almost all of the *Didache* in its chapter 7, adds "presbyters" at this point in its text, thus indicating the three-fold ministry of the fourth century and later (*Apostolic Consititutions* 7.31). There is no mention of deaconesses in this chapter, although they undoubtedly existed from apostolic times (Rom. 16:1; 1 Tim. 3:11?).

As has been mentioned, the overseers in the NT and in the *Didache* are identical with the presbyters. There were always several presbyter-overseers in one congregation and constituted what is called today the "presbytery." In addition to *Phil.* 1:1, consider *Acts* 14:23: "And when they had appointed (same word as in 15:1) elders for them in every church, with prayer and fasting they committed them to the Lord in whom they had believed."

The identity of overseers and presbyters that we find in the *Didache* is further found in the so-called *First Epistle of Clement* to Rome, universally located also in the first century. He mentions "overseers and deacons," commends obedience to presbyters without mentioning "overseers," and calls the office of the Corinthian presbyters the "episcopate" (42, 44, 57). *Hermas* also refers to overseers and deacons, but does not mention a threefold division of a single overseer along with presbyters and deacons below him (*Hermas* 13. 1). The situation that prevails in *Ignatius* is the authority of a single ἐπίσκοπος over a church, although not yet diocesan, but simply as the head of a single church along with its presbyters and deacons. This arrangement is simply not evident in the NT and the other douments from the first century.

> By and by as the Apostles, Prophets and Evangelists disappeared, the Bishops absorbed all the higher offices and functions, and became in the estimation of the Church the successors of the Apostles; while the Presbyters became the Priests, and the Deacons became the Levites in the new Christian Catholic hierarchy.[122]

Chapter Nine

The Theology of the *Didache*

To some the title of this chapter may appear to be self-defeating. Dissenting voices will be raised against the possibility of finding much theological reflection in the *Didache*. Sometimes they say that what theology that may be found there is rather "thin."[123] I beg to differ, but I must be honest about declaring that the theology of the Didache does not jump out and grab the casual reader. The book is a handbook for those who have found life in the Lord's Servant and about how that life should be manifested in the assembly of fellow believers. It is not a manual of theology. While we must acknowledge its limitations in this regard, we should not be blind to seeing what is really there, if we dig deep enough to perceive it.

My contention is that the theology of the Didache is more implicit than explicit. It is there, undergirding the moral and spiritual paranesis, but only manifesting itself at certain explicit points in the text. I am convinced that the message of the book, which I acknowledge is largely ethical, cannot be understood clearly unless we discern the theological undergirding which causes the advice offered to make sense to the new convert.

With that as an introduction, it is important to offer a few general comments before we attempt to outline the proposed theological grid that I believe underlies the book. Many have observed that the world view of the book is very Jewish Christian in both its general and specific points. It is hard to deny that the author himself was a Jewish Christian, although he writes to help converts from the Gentile world to assimilate into their new fellowship of faith. But he does not invite them to enter a purely Jewish community. He realizes that the hope of Israel has been fulfilled in the Lord's servant, Jesus, and that he has given us life and knowledge through the "good news" of his person and work. This is particularly evident in the eucharistic prayers of chapter 9 and 10, which we will consider in more detail later in his chapter.

The church historian, Philip Schaff offers this able summary of the book's theological message.

> Christianity appears in the Didache as a pure and holy life based upon the teaching and example of Christ and on the Decalogue as explained by him in the Sermon on the Mount, and summed up in the royal law of love to God and man. The Didache agrees in the respect with the Epistle of James, the Epistle of Polycarp, and the writings of Justin martyr (who, however, already branched out into philosophical speculation). The younger Pliny describes the Christians in Bithynia as scrupulously moral and conscientious worshippers of Christ. It was by the practical proof of virtue and piety more than by doctrines that the Christian religion conquered the heathen world. And to this day a living Christian is the best apology for Christianity.[124]

It is true that the book largely echoes only the Synoptic Gospels. It does not reflect the theological depth of a Paul or a John. It even lags behind the doctrinal content of some of the other post-Apostolic writings, such as the Clements, Ignatius and Diognetus. But we must not infer too much from these omissions, especially when we consider the genre of the book. Silence does not imply opposition, nor even ignorance. While there are many doctrines that may be taken for granted, other doctrines are touched upon, but only as they relate to the immensely practical purpose of the book. The book was not intended to be exhaustive, and was only one of other means of instruction and edification. The book itself mentions that further instruction takes place in the assembly by those who teach the word of God (4:1), and it is assumed that arriving teachers will bring further "instruction about righteousness and the knowledge of the Lord" to the congregation (11:1, 2).

Because of the Jewish Christian orientation of the author, there have been occasional attempts to charge the *Didache* with Ebionism.[125] In response to this accusation, the simple fact is that the Didache shows no trace of the chief characteristics of the Judaizing heresy of Ebionism: the necessity of circumcision for salvation, the perpetual obligation of the ceremonial as we all the moral Torah, the denial of the Deity of Jesus, and the intense hostility to Paul as an apostate and heretic. One must read these teachings between the lines and even into the lines to charge the Didachist with Ebionism.

The history of early Jewish Christianity is pock-marked by scholarly mine fields containing serious chronological gaps and the sometimes contradictory ancient descriptions by the heresiologists. Furthermore, the uncritical acceptance of the Walter Bauer hypothesis of early Christianity has caused some scholars to write about this matter with far more of a social and theological agenda than should characterize the history of this unique phenomenon in the church's history.[126] One of the greatest sins in this regard is an anachronistic reading back into such documents as the *Didache* the teachings that characterized Jewish Christian sects of the third and fourth centuries. Fortunately, most *Didache* scholars have avoided these tendencies and have studied the document on its own merit without using it to push their own pet theory of how the early years of

Christianity developed. Yet, that theological tendenz remains, not only for the *Didache*, but for other documents of the early Church.

With those caveats serving as an introduction, what can we say about the theological substructure of the *Didache*? I structure the following presentation along the lines of the familiar grid of the theological loci communes, more for a convenient paradigm than by assuming that the Didachist would have thought in these categories. Thus, we shall try to summarize what the book expressly or implicitly teaches about God, Christ, the Holy Spirit, Man, the Church and Sacraments, and Last Things.

God

God is the Creator—"you will love the God who made you" (1:2). He is the Almighty Ruler who made all things—"You, almighty Master, created all things for the sake of your name "(10:3). He is our "Father in heaven" (8:2). His Providence extends to all events in our lives—"You will accept the experiences that happen to you as good things, knowing that, apart from God, nothing happens." He is the Giver of all good gifts, temporal and spiritual, the Author of our salvation, the object of prayer and praise (prayers in chs. 9 and 10). To him belongs all glory forever, through Jesus Christ (8:2; 9:4; 10:4).

Christ

Jesus is Lord and Savior (10:2, 3), God's Servant and God's Son (9:2). He is the Author of the Gospel (8:2; 15:4). He is spiritually present in the Church and will visibly come again to judgment (16:1, 7, 8). Through Him knowledge and eternal life have been made known to us ((9:3; 10:2). He is identified with the Yahweh of the Old Testament—"The Lord will come and all the holy ones with him" (16:7, applying Zech. 14:5 to him).

At this point, it is necessary to draw out more the title that the Didachist gives to Jesus in the Eucharistic prayers. Note the following excerpts from the prayers in chapters 9 and 10:

9:2 First, concerning the cup: We give you thanks, our Father,
   For the holy vine of your servant David
   Which you revealed to us through your servant Jesus.
   To you is the glory forever.
9:3 And concerning the broken bread: We give you thanks, our Father,
   For the life and knowledge,
   Which you revealed to us through your servant Jesus.
   To you is the glory forever.
10:3 You, almighty Master,
   Created all things for the sake of your name,
   Both food and drink you have given to people for enjoyment
      in order that they might give thanks.
   But to us you have graciously bestowed spiritual food and drink
      and eternal life through your **servant**.

Three times the prayer refers to Jesus as God's "servant." The Greek word is παις—the same word that the LXX uses to translate the Isaianic עבד (41:8, 9; 42:1; 44:21; 52:13). In this way, the Didachist embodies the confession of faith of the earliest Jewish believers that Jesus was that promised "servant of the Lord" who would corporately represent Israel and succeed where they failed (49:3-5). The fact that the LXX also utilizes the Greek word douloj for that same עבד should not divert us from the fact that Jesus also identified Himself with that Isaianic servant. He did this explicitly in Luke 22:37, "For I tell you that this Scripture must be fulfilled in me: 'And he was numbered with the transgressors.' For what is written about me has its fulfillment."

Oscar Cullman has traced this title of Jesus through its use in Judaism, the New Testament and the early church. He offers this observation on the application of the concept by Jesus in his own Messianic self-consciousness.

> Besides this single direct quotation (i.e., Luke 22:37), however, there are a number of allusions to Isa. 52-53 which can hardly be questioned as such. The clearest are in the sayings of Jesus about the Lord's Supper. They indicates clearly, that the thought of Isa. 53 also lies behind most of the passages we have mentioned above in which Jesus speaks more generally about the necessity of his death. We need not compare the four versions of Jesus' institutions of the Lord's Supper handed down to us in Mark 14.24, Matt. 26.28, Luke 22.20, and 1 Cor. 11.24. All four passages agree in the most important point: when Jesus distributed the supper, he announced that he would shed his blood *for many*. It is all the more remarkable that not only Paul but also all three Synoptics in relating the story of the Last Supper recall that Jesus at this decisive moment ascribed to himself the role of the *ebed Yahweh*.[127]

Further evidence of Jesus' application of the Isaianic servant to himself is his statement in *Mark* 10:45, "The Son of Man came not to be served but to serve, and to give his life as a ransom for many"—a clear allusion to *Isa.* 53:5. Cullman cites other evidence but since it is so abundant, we will not tarry here to cite it all. Only a radical redactional criticism attempts to explain away all of this evidence both form the lips of Jesus bit also from John the Baptist (*John* 1:29) and from the gospel writers themselves.

The *Acts of the Apostles* offers the strongest evidence that the most ancient Christianity offered an explanation of the person and work of Jesus which could be characterized as an *ebed Yahweh* Christology. Cullmann coined the term, "Paidology" to express this connection with the Isaianic παῖς.[128] The account of the conversion of the Ethiopian eunuch (8:26 ff.) indicates that in the first century Jesus was explicitly identified with the παῖς of Isaiah 53. The actual title appears four times in Acts, and all four in the same section, the description of the earliest Jerusalem witness. In Peter's second sermon, delivered under Solomon's Portico in the Temple, he twice refers to Jesus as the παῖς του θεού.

The God of Abraham, the God of Isaac, and the God of Jacob, the God of our fathers, glorified his **servant** Jesus, whom you delivered over and denied in the presence of Pilate, when he had decided to release him (3:13). God, having raised up his **servant**, sent him to you first, to bless you by turning every one of you from your wickedness (3:26).

It is interesting to note that Peter, who uttered the above words, was involved in the only other two occasions when παῖς is directly used of Jesus in the NT – in the very next chapter of Acts when the disciples gathered with Peter pray as follows.

For truly in this city there were gathered together against your holy **servant** Jesus, whom you anointed, both Herod and Pontius Pilate, along with the Gentiles and the peoples of Israel (4:27). . . .while you stretch out your hand to heal, and signs and wonders are performed through the name of your holy **servant** Jesus (4:30).

Cullmann concludes, "This confirms the existence of a very old Christology on the basis of which Jesus is called the ebed Yahweh. The Christology later disappears, but it must extend back to the very early period of the Christian faith."[129] Furthermore, while Peter was involved with these four uses of the παῖς Christology, in his first epistle he cites the passages from Isaiah which relate to the *ebed Yahweh*.

For to this you have been called, because Christ also suffered for you, leaving you an example, so that you might follow in his steps. He committed no sin, neither was deceit found in his mouth. When he was reviled, he did not revile in return; when he suffered, he did not threaten, but continued entrusting himself to him who judges justly. He himself bore our sins in his body on the tree, that we might die to sin and live to righteousness. By his wounds you have been healed. For you were straying like sheep, but have now returned to the Shepherd and Overseer of your souls (1 Peter 2:21-25).

I believe, on the basis of these texts, that the *ebed Yahweh* "Paidology" dominated the Christology of the Apostle Peter. Cullmann again expresses his conclusion to all of this quite effectively.

He, who had wanted to divert Jesus from the way of suffering (Matt. 16:22), who had denied him at the decisive moment of the passion story, would be the first after Easter to grasp the necessity of the offence. He could not express his conviction better than with the designation *ebed Yahweh*, especially since he must have known what great importance Jesus himself had attributed to the ideas related to it. Subsequent periods of the Church were often unjust to Paul by placing him in the shadow of Peter. Are we not perhaps unjust to Peter when we place him in the shadow of Paul?[130]

Now what does the relevance of all this information about the use of παῖς in the NT have to our study of Christology in the *Didache*? The specific title, "Jesus the Servant of God," soon was forced into the background. It does not appear anywhere in the later sections of the New Testament (although the concept of a suffering Messiah certainly does). It was, however, maintained longest in the documents which preserve the oldest elements of Christianity: *the ancient liturgies*, part of which we have already quoted in *Didache* 9 and 10. I also find it fascinating that just as Peter referred to David in his pre-messianic role as God's servant (Acts 4:25), so the Didachist also mentions David in that same pre-messianic role as God's servant (9:2). Furthermore, in the oldest liturgy of the Roman church (*1 Clement* 59:3-61:3), Jesus is referred to as God's "beloved servant" (59:2-4). Peter's presence in Rome is well known. Could we also be witnessing his influence in the Antiochene church as well?

Two implications of this "Paidology" in the *Didache* must be noted at this point. This theology again points to the antiquity of the *Didache*, whose Christology went all the way back to the earliest Jewish-Christian days of the church. This helps to date the *Didache*, or at least the eucharistic prayers found in it, to the most primitive foundational period of the Jewish Christian church. If nothing else, it definitely makes any second century date highly questionable. In my own opinion, it is more evidence of a pre-70 origin. The second implication is directed to a number of modern scholars who have affirmed that there is no sacrificial language in the *Didache*'s Eucharistic prayers. They think that this is contrary to the Eucharistic prayers found in the Synoptics and in Paul, which contain words of institution that clearly are sacrificial in tone (e.g., *1 Cor.* 11). When we recognize, however, that the language of Jesus as God's παῖς undoubtedly evokes the larger context of Isaiah 52:13-53:12, then the concept of a suffering and redemptive Servant/Messiah becomes implicit in the language of the prayers.

Holy Spirit and Trinity

The Spirit is associated with the Father and the Son—"After you have said all these things beforehand, immerse in the name of the Father and of the Son and of the Holy Spirit in flowing water" (7:1). "And if you should not have either, pour out water onto the head three times in the name of the Father and of the Son and of the Holy Spirit (7:3). This is the earliest and also strongest text to illustrate the belief in the doctrine that would later be called the Trinity.

But there are other references that teach the salvific activity of the Spirit. In a passage with remarkable theological implications, the Didachist is counseling kind treatment of slaves who belong to a Christian master. He then he gives the following as a reason, "For He does not come to call according to social status, but those whom the Spirit has prepared" (4:10). While the purpose of the statement is profoundly practical, the theological grounding for it is as profound as any later Calvinistic theology could express.

Finally, the Spirit speaks through the prophets, and sins against the Holy Spirit will not be forgiven—"And every prophet speaking in the Spirit you should not test nor judge, for every sin will be forgiven, but this sin will not be forgiven" (11:7).

Man

Man is made in the image of God (5:2), but he is sinful and he needs forgiveness (8:2). He must confess his transgressions to receive pardon (4:14; 14:1, 2). Man's duty is to love God and his neighbor and to show this practically by abstaining from all sins of thought, word and deed, and by observing the commandments (1:6). This also must be done in accord with the Gospel (11:3), neither adding nor taking away anything from those sacred scriptures (4:13). "This is the Way of Life, but the way of sin is the Way of Death. There is no third way, no compromise between good and evil, between life and death."[131]

I offer no separate category for "Soteriology," because the Didachist does not frame the issues of salvation in the categories that are familiar to later generations. One writer, upset at the strong statement on almsgiving in 4:6, thinks that the NT doctrine of grace is foreign to this writing.[132] The verse goes, "If you should have something through the work of your hands, you will give it as a ransom for your sins." Statements can certainly be found in Second Temple Jewish literature that support a connection between charitable giving and forgiveness (*Tobit* 4:10 and *Testament of Zebulun* 8, e.g.). What may be surprising is that this strong Jewish tradition may have its root in canonical Jewish writings. Prov. 16: 6 states, "By steadfast love (חֶסֶד)and faithfulness (אֱמֶת) iniquity is atoned for, and by the fear of the LORD one turns away from evil." Can free grace also be found here? Or consider Daniel's advice to Nebuchadnezzar in Dan. 4:27 (LXX, 4:24), "Therefore, O king, let my counsel be acceptable to you: break off your sins by practicing righteousness (צִדְקָה), and your iniquities by showing mercy (מְחַן) to the oppressed."

In my opinion, too much has been made of this statement by the Didachist in a modern desire to make him express Christian faith and belief in the terminology of the Protestant Reformation. I think our author would be in agreement with James when he writes, "Show me your faith apart from your works, and I will show you my faith by my works" (*James* 2:18).

The Church

Attention has already been given to both the sacraments (chapter 7) and the ministers (chapter 8) in the *Didache*. But in what has often been termed a church manual, we expect and also find more theological discussion about the church. This especially takes place in those richly theological prayers in chapters nine and ten. The church is God's instrument in bringing in the kingdom which He had prepared for her. He will deliver her from all evil andperfect her in his love (9:4; 10:5). All true Christians are really one although they are scattered over the world. God will eventually gather them from the four winds into his kingdom (10:5).

Despite its Jewish background the *Didache* teaches that the "Lord's day," which can only be Sunday according to the clear usage of the word,[133] should be kept as a day of worship and thanksgiving (14:1). The Lord's prayer should be repeated thrice daily (8:2), and Wednesday and Friday should be given to fasting (8:1). Finally, reverence and sacrificial gratitude are due to the ministers of Christ:"And everyone coming in the name of the Lord, let him be received; and then, having put him to the test, you will know, for you will have understanding of right and left. If, on the one hand, the one coming is passing through, help him as much as you are able. He will not remain, however, among you except for two or three days, if there should be a need" (13:1, 2; also 4:1; 11:1, 4; 12:1).

Before we consider the last category of theology, it may be good to offer the following observations. If one still objects to the lack of theology in the *Didache*, I observe that it may be difficult to find more theology in the *Epistle of James*. Neither of them is guilty of Ebionism, because both antedate that stunted and impoverished heresy of later years. Rather, they both represent an early Jewish-Christian type of teaching, before the breadth and depth of Pauline theology burst onto the scene. They teach a plain, common-sense type of Christianity, not dogmatical but ethical, not very profound but eminently practical, and even now that might be suited to the taste of some very devout believers. "We cannot disregard it as long as the *Epistle of James* keeps its place in the canon of the New Testament."[134]

Last Things

Since nearly an entire chapter of the *Didache* is devoted to eschatology, it is important to note that the first eschatological notes are sounded in the eucaharistic prayers. As just one example, note 10:5, "Remember, Lord, your church, to save her from every evil, and to perfect her in your love, and to gather her together from the four winds, the sanctified into your kingdom which you have prepared for her." Such an emphasis is consistent, for example, with the words of institution in *Luke* 22:16, "And he said to them, "I have earnestly desired to eat this Passover with you before I suffer.For I tell you I will not eat it until it is fulfilled in the kingdom of God." The Pauline form also looks ahead, as he wrote in *1 Cor.* 11:26, "For as often as you eat this bread and drink the cup, you proclaim the Lord's death until he comes."

In an insightful article on the eschatology of the Apostolic Fathers, F. F. Bruce comments on the use of *Maranatha* in 10:6:

> The invocation *Maranatha* ("Our Lord, come!") goes back to the early Aramaic-speaking phase of the church's life, and (like *Hosanna, Amen,* and *Alleluia*) was taken over into the Greek-speaking churches untranslated (cf. 1 Cor. 16:22, where also we may have a primitive versicle and response).[135]

When we consider that most of the the final chapter is centered on eschatological themes, it is surprising to discover that so little has been written about the role this specific chapter plays overall doctrine of the "Last Things." The two standard collections of scholarly writings on the Didache do contain articles on individual issues related to chapter sixteen.[136] In his larger commentary, Milavec does devote over seventy pages to explain various issues in the chapter. Nothing has been written, however, that approaches the thoroughness of the (unfortunately) unpublished dissertation of George Eldon Ladd in 1949.[137]

Before we consider the details of the chapter and also interact with Ladd's conclusions, we will present the chapter in an analytical translation for easy reference.

16:1   [A] Be watchful over your life;
           [1] do not let your lamps be quenched,
           [2] and do not let your waists be ungirded.
       [B] But be prepared,
       for you do not know the hour in which our Lord is coming.

16:2   [C] And frequently be gathered together,
           seeking what is appropriate for your souls;
           for the whole time of your faith will not benefit you
           unless you are perfected in the last time.

16:3   [1] For, in the last days
           [a] the false prophets and corrupters will be multiplied,
           [b] and the sheep will be turned into wolves,
           [c] and the love will be turned into hatred.

16:4   For, when lawlessness increases,
             [a] they will hate each other
             [b] and they will persecute
             [c] and they will betray each other.

       [2] And then will appear the world-deceiver as a son of God,
           [a] and he will do signs and wonders,
           [b] and the earth will be delivered into his hands,
           [c] and he will do unlawful things
             that never have happened from eternity.

16:5   [3] Then the human creation will come
             into the fiery test,
           [a] and many will be led into sin and will perish,
           [b] but the ones remaining firm in their faith,
             will be saved by the curse itself.

16:6   [4] And then the signs of the truth will appear:
           [a] first, a sign of an opening in heaven,
           [b] then a sign of a trumpet sound,
           [c] and the third [sign will be] a resurrection of dead ones--

16:7   but not of all [the dead],
               but as it was said:
             "The Lord will come and all the holy ones with him."

16:8   [5] Then the world will see the Lord coming atop the clouds
            of heaven . . .

It is quite common for writers to refer to this chapter as an "apocalypse."
Hans Seeliger, however, has clarified, in light of a generally accepted definition
of the "apocalyptic" genre during this period, that *Didache* 16 does not actually-
qualify as an apocalyptic text.[138] He cites John J. Collins as defining an "apocalypse" as follows:

> "Apocalypse" is a genre of revelatory literature with a narrative framework, in
> which a revelation is mediated by an otherworldly being to a human recipient,
> disclosing a transcendent reality which is both temporal, insofar as it envisages
> eschatological salvation, and spatial, insofar as it involves another, supernatural
> world.[139]

In light of this definition, it is important to note that in this chapter there is
no narrative framework, no revealer nor receiver of an apocalyptic message, no
information about the manner of the revelation, and nothing is revealed in the
sense of an "unveiling." What is already known is repeated for the deepening of
knowledge. In other words, the Didachist may have been influenced by apocalyptic sources, but he does not claim to be a channel of an apocalyptic unveiling
of revelation. Seeliger's thesis about the chapter is worthy of serious consideration. "The apocalyptic conclusion of the *Didache*, directed against false prophets, preserves an important part of the preaching of the prophets attested in the
Didache."[140] This makes good sense in light of the fact that the previous instruction in the book, particularly the "two ways" section, must have been taught
often until it was written down in this form. Perhaps the material in this chapter
was taught by prophets and now is written for the instruction of the catechumens
and all who will learn form it.

The chapter opens with an intense three-fold exhortation: 1) "be watchful"
2) "be prepared" and 3) "be gathered together." With these imperatives, there is
only one indicative statement that serves to be the basis for the three admonitions: "for you do not know the hour in which our Lord is coming." Then follows the details of this coming with a series of future indicative statements in
16:3-8, with no further imperatives. We do not know if there originally were
additional exhortations following 16:8 since it probably is not the original ending—more on that anon.

The reference to being "perfected in the last time" recalls the other reference to being "perfect" in 6:2. Either a careful redactor or the original author
(my preference) skillfully placed these references at the beginning and the end
of this second main section of the book to serve as an inclusio that frames this
part of his literary discourse.

These urgent exhortations are in light of what must have been considered an
imminent coming of the Lord, and they are consistent with similar exhortations

in the NT in light of the *parousia* (Matt. 24:42-44; Luke 12:35; 1 Thess. 15-18; 2 Pet. 3, etc.). Many writers have affirmed, especially in the first period of *Didache* research, that Matthew's "Olivet Discourse" and especially 24:42 must have influenced the writer in these verses. This is not the place to re-enter that discussion, which has already taken place in chapter five. The current scholarly preference is that here and elsewhere he utilized Jesus tradition that was still primarily oral and that he was not using any proto-canonical writings. My own opinion is that the Didachist is here and throughout the chapter influenced by what he also calls the "Gospel of our Lord," a Greek translation of Matthew's *logia*. I also conclude that, whatever sources he may or may not have used, he adapted them and shaped them into this form for his own purposes

There is an intensely practical purpose that the Didachist has in all this: the preparation of his readers for the difficulties of the end. The "World Deceiver" or ὁ κοσμοπλανὴς (a title coined by the Didachist?) will shortly appear as a false son of God and will deceive the entire earth by claiming divine powers. The one way to withstand these troubles is by faithful attendance at the Christian gatherings. He urges his readers to faithfulness so that they will not be among those who turn away.

Much speculation has centered on the identity of the "curse" in 16:5b: "but the ones remaining firm in their faith will be saved by the curse itself." The word is καταθέμα, one of a number of words that can mean "curse."[141] The word does not occur in the LXX and appears in the NT only as a preferred variant reading in *Rev.* 22:3. One would desire that the statement by Paul in *Gal.* 3:13 might use this word: "Christ redeemed us from the curse of the law by becoming a curse for us-for it is written, 'Cursed is everyone who is hanged on a tree'," but the "curse" there is κατάρα. In light of the lack of any exact parallels, Schaff comments, "This is the most difficult passage (in the Didache) next to 'the cosmic mystery' in XI. 11." Even in 1887 he mentions at least seven interpretations of the word.[142] It is probably still best, in light of Deut. 21:23, (despite the different Greek word), that this 16:5 is a paradoxical statement that the "cursed one" (i.e., Jesus) will save the faithful from the eschatological curse, because he already experienced it by being cursed by God. Probably the Didachist had *Deut.* 21:23 in mind and simply used another word.

The three "signs of the truth" that he describes in 16:6, 7 have similarities to Matthew's discourse but also differences. He mentions an "opening in heaven," which could be simply a preparation of the sky for the later appearing of the Lord (16:8). Some scholars, however, have translated the word ἐκπετάσεως as a "spreading out," signifying a celestial "sign of the cross" being displayed.[143] The "trumpet" echoes (pardon the pun) the same sound in *Matt.* 24:31; *1 Cor.* 15:52; and *1 Thess.*4:16. To think that the Didachist, however, is referencing any Pauline statement is simply not valid. Paul and the Didachist were probably both echoing an original statement of "the Lord."

The final sign, "a resurrection of dead ones," should not surprise Bible readers familiar with the apocalyptic Daniel's statement in 12:2: "And many of those who sleep in the dust of the earth shall awake, some to everlasting life, and some to shame and everlasting contempt." What we do not expect, however, is that the Didachist limits this resurrection. He adds, "but not of all [the dead]" and then quotes Zech. 14:5, applying the "holy ones' in that passage to "saints" not angels. From the earliest commentators down to more current times, this has been taken as indicating the chiliasm, or millennarianism of the author.[144] Since Barnabas, Papias, Justin Martyr, Irenaeus and Tertullian were pronounced chiliasts, we should not be surprised if the Didachist was one. There are reasons, however, to be careful about dogmatism in this matter. The resurrection could possibly be for believers only and would not demand another later resurrection of unbelievers. The book ends abruptly at 16:8 with no further mention of any sort of future kingdom, earthly or heavenly. Finally, Rev. 20 is the first writing to mention the thousand years as the length of the future earthly kingdom and the Didachist wrote prior to that book.

This brings us to the end of the book, which just about all, including Leon the scribe, believe was not the original ending. It has already been mentioned that the scribe indicates by the blank lines following 16:8 in his manuscript that his *vorlage* also did not contain anything beyond these words and that this was not the original ending. Since the *Apostolic Constitutions* and other works that incorporate the *Didache* do have additional words at this point, scholars have speculated if these works may contain the original ending. Most scholars today view the solution proposed by Robert E. Aldridge as the most probable. He suggests that a combination of Constitution's ending and that of the Georgian version "may be accepted as the proximate true ending."[145] However, I would like to offer my own solution as a variation of Aldridge's. Since part of Constitution's ending is very clearly a borrowing of Paul's statement about the glorious eschaton in *1 Cor.* 2:9, I offer the ending without that insertion which I am sure that the original Didachist would not have used. Thus after 16:8 would be the following words:

> . . . with the angels of His power, in the throne of His kingdom, to condemn the devil, the deceiver of the world, and to render to everyone according to his deeds. Then shall the wicked go away into everlasting punishment, but the righteous shall enter eternal life. And they shall rejoice in the kingdom of God, which is in Christ Jesus.

One last word about chapter sixteen and especially about its ending. In his dissertation, Ladd presents an argument that the abbreviated ending of the chapter 16 may not have been accidental, but rather deliberate. While not being dogmatic, he suggests that the original ending of *Didache* may have contained a clear reference to an earthly kingdom following the resurrection of the righteous dead and preceding a resurrection of the wicked dead after that kingdom. By the third century, when chiliasm had fallen out of favor with many segments of the "Great Church," the original chiliastic ending was then stricken and its more generic ending left. What appeared in the *Apostolic Constitutions* and the Georgian version thus was a doctored ending that omitted the chiliastic reference in favor of a view more amenable to the church at that time, even adding the Pauline statement from *1 Cor.* 2:9 for good effect.[146]

While Ladd's suggestion is made without claiming any certainty, it lacks in one important matter that should counsel caution in accepting it. If the original ending was stricken to avoid any chiliastic implications, why didn't this editor add another ending in its place and not leave the ending hanging as it so clearly appears to be?

While the *Didache* certainly does not qualify as a handbook on theology, enough theology can be seen in it to conclude that its moral imperatives rest on an implicit set of theological indicatives.

Chapter Ten

The Lessons of the *Didache*

This final chapter is an effort on my part to see what value this little book may have for the life of the church today. It is neither a summary of my book nor of my conclusions about the various issues that are raised in its study. It contains my own observations about the lessons that I think it contains for Christians today who want to "do church" and who believe that the earliest Christians may have something to tell us about that task. In that regard, it is more personal than the other chapters, but the conclusions arise from some serious wrestling with this little book over a period of ten years. So, what have I learned from this study of the Didache?

1. In spite of my enthusiasm for the book, I have learned that the *Didache* has no more authority for me than any other post-Apostolic writing. This may calm the fears expressed among some of my evangelical friends. While it does claim to pass on the teaching of the apostles, it does not come to me with the force of an apostolic letter. Its authority is derived, not directly from God in a revelation, but only in passing on what the Lord and his apostles have already taught. Recently, I heard a *Didache* scholar argue that the book should be received into the New Testament canon someday. I hold no such hopes. It value is historical and historical only. But its value, in my opinion, exceeds that of any other post-Apostolic document. The *Didache* provides a window into the life of the early church like no other work does. It shows me what at least one section of the early church was like. I know the difference between canonical literature and literature like this. But even the inspired works of the Bible do not tell me everything I would like to know about what the nascent church felt was important and therefore stressed. There are gaps in the record of the *Acts of the Apostles*. The epistles fill in some of those. The *Didache* helps to fill in more of them for me.

2. From the first six chapters of the *Didache*, I have learned that the earliest church put a high value on instruction for young converts before their baptism. In my own ecclesiastical circle, we do not use the word "catechumen." Some of my friends who read my use of the word may wonder what this terminology is all about. We call these sessions "baptismal classes" or "church membership classes" or "fundamentals of the faith." We still don't know exactly how these ancient periods of instruction were carried on—weekly, at nights, on Lord's Day post-meetings? But in the *Didache* we do discover what was communicated as "the apostles' doctrine" in Acts 4:32. As I read and re-read chapters 1-5, I am struck by the level of moral and ethical content in this teaching. The absence of clearly expressed doctrinal tenets impresses itself on me. Yet I know that behavior without a basis lapses into moralism. The basic faith and facts about the Gospel and the role of Jesus must have been assumed to some degree. But even with an understanding that theology is more implied than expressed, I think that the strongly practical tone of the chapters means that the practical Christian life was stressed more than we do in our classes. Go to one of our baptismal or foundations classes and most of what you hear will be the basics of doctrinal truths about God, Jesus, the Holy Spirit, salvation and the nature of the Bible itself. With our stress on right doctrine, have we assumed that people will know how to apply that doctrine in the everyday decisions of their lives? Have we sold some Christians a bill of goods in making them think that as long as they hold the right beliefs that good behavior will automatically follow? Why do Christians with good doctrine still face real problems for which they have no practical answers? Has our teaching been faulty in addressing their heads but neglecting their hearts? The moral tone of the teaching in the *Didache* has much to challenge us about rethinking and retooling our baptismal or catechumen classes. With the right framework of theology in place, we sorely need instruction in the purity, gentleness, humility and charity that should mark the Christian life. The superior morality of early Christianity carried in it the guarantee of its ultimate victory.

As I write this, Amish families in Pennsylvania have just buried their own children who were murdered in a horrible action in their simple schoolhouse. The forgiving attitude of these families who suffered so much and yet reached out to the killer's family has astounded the onlooking world. People have learned far more about Christianity as they observed these gentle Christians' behavior than from hearing many doctrinal sermons.

3. I have learned from the *Didache* that the sacraments of baptism and the eucharist, or as we prefer to call it, "the Lords Supper," played a much larger role in the life of their church than they do in mine. Baptism was the culmination of a process of conversion and instruction. It was not so separated from one's profession of faith that we wonder today if it is really important since it is not part of our salvation. We often make such a bifurcation between faith and baptism out of fear that we may lapse into sacramentalism and that dreaded curse we call baptismal regeneration. Why are there so many who have never been baptized? Could it be because we have given the impression that it is so separate from faith that it is really optional? The idea of an unbaptized Christian was simply not entertained in the New Testament and the earliest church. I am not implying that there is no need for some delay so that proper instruction should take place. But the catechumens should know that baptism is part and parcel of becoming a Christian. The *Didache* is clear that no unbaptized persons should partake of that which is the right and privilege of every Christian – partaking of the eucharist. The stress in chapter seven on the meaning of baptism rather than on its form is a healthy one. We are so concerned that we get them fully submerged – and the *Didache* teaches that too – that we fuss and fight about the proper mode while missing the most important issue: that we are uniting with the Savior in his death and resurrection. We who are Baptists, whether we bear that specific name or not, need the *Didache* to remind us that immersion in a warm and comfortable tank is not the pattern of the early church. But we also need its teaching to remind us that circumstances may not always allow the ideal—immersion three times in cold, running water. Fussy Baptists and strict Presbyterians both need ato learn a lesson from the example of pastoral genius that underlies this book. Finally—and this is challenging for one who has never practiced baptism this way—the pattern of trine immersion was not recommended only by the *Didache*. It was the practice of the early church in all regions until the third century—and it is still the practice of the eastern churches. When will we who are so loud in our cries of *sola scriptura*, realize that the phrase did not mean that only Scripture was to be read. It meant that Scripture is our only final authority. But if two hundred years' worth of Christians read their Bible as teaching trine immersion, shouldn't we ask if we have been reading our Bible correctly if we insist on single immersion only?

Now concerning (περι δε!) the eucharist, as the Didachist would say. It is clear from this book, as it should have been clear from the New Testament and also from other early Christian writings that believers celebrated the eucharist weekly - not monthly or quarterly or yearly! For fear that it may become rote we do it as rarely as we can get away with it. We stress that Paul said "as often as you do it" as if that expression means that there is no pattern ever provided about the frequency of its observance. We shouldn't need early Christian writings to remind us of this as the *Acts* and *1 Corinthians* are pretty clear in this regard. But if through millennium and a half years, Christians all read their Bibles as teaching a weekly observance, why do we think that we got smart about this practice in the last few years? We suffer from a case of historical amnesia and the worst case of it is in the evangelical church. And that amnesia is never so badly demonstrated as in how we observe the sacraments. If someone fears that I am for turning the church back to a Roman mass, they only have to read the simple liturgy in *Didache* 9 and 10 to know that Rome desperately needs to read and heed those chapters too.

4. I have learned from the *Didache* that church leadership on the local level that consists of spiritual overseers and deacons is the best pattern of church governance. Now I recognize that this book was written when apostles and prophets were still itinerating, because the situation described was still during the New Testament period. I know that we cannot put in place the exact model of ecclesiology that is exemplified in the *Didache*. Even the book itself appears to recognize that this period is coming to a close soon. But the pattern that is exemplified in the New Testament appears also to be the same as the one so described by the Didachist. Frequent gatherings of believers under the leadership of godly and righteous leaders for instruction in the word the Lord and for sharing the eucharist is not far from what we see today. Or is it? The emphasis on market driven philosophies of church growth seems so alien to what was done in the first century. Today we emphasize what people should come to church to get, and how we can supply what they want so we can best service them. The simplicity, integrity and quiet holiness that pervades the *Didache* is absent from so many of our church efforts today. When have you last heard brothers and sisters confessing their sins in a church meeting? We seem to think that such a practice is too dangerous and open to abuse to even encourage it. Spiritual leaders of course should oversee such things and channel them into godly paths. But taking the "safe" path is not always the path to God's blessing. I know enough about the history of revivals to know that many of them have begun when public confession of sins began to take place.

The Didachist reminds the new believers that the congregation can nourish and support them and they will find what is beneficial for their lives in frequent gatherings, and thus move toward maturity and perfection in their lives. Many decry the church for being the last place where reality can be seen. We put up our facades and dare not open ourselves up publicly—for whatever fearful reasons we have. Honesty and integrity are rarely seen in our prayer requests, for example. As I read this little book, I am called back to a time of simplicity and reality that I so miss – or maybe have never even experienced.

5. Lastly and briefly, **I have learned from the Didache that living eschatologically means far more than knowing my prophetic charts and having my end-time scenario down to the year, month and day!** It means living in a constant awareness that because of the work of Jesus I am living in the end times now and I still anticipate that the consummation could be very near. I am remnded of the saying that prophecy is given to us not so we can form a calendar but so we can form a character. Prayerfulness, watchfulness, honesty, and holiness should be the effect in my life of knowing about the "last things." The reader may respond, "Well, I am aware of all that from my reading of the New Testament." That is fine, but it is also good to be reminded that others very near to the apostles approached eschatology in such a practical way.

I believe that Milavec's brief summary of the book's unity is helpful and expresses very well my own judgement.

> Upon inspection, therefore, the *Didache* exhibits a remarkable unity and purpose. It opens by offering the candidate the key orientation toward love of God and love of neighbor that characterize the Way of Life. It closes by evoking the expectation of that glorious day when the Lord God will come atop the clouds of heaven (16:8) and gather into the kingdom those whose lives have exhibited

this orientation. Thus the *Didache* traces how humble beginnings anticipate an exalted end.[146]

In all honesty, however, when I compare the content of this plain and simple little tract to the depth and breadth of something like the Pauline writings, I am thankful even more for the full canonical revelation of the New Testament. While the *Didache* is neither the last nor the best word on these subjects, it is a word that should be heard again—after too long a silence!

A message that I heard just as I was finishing the rough draft of this book reminded me of one of the lasting lessons that I have taken from the study of the *Didache*. The pastor said that God attends our church when, in the terms of *Isaiah* 66:2, we "tremble" at His word. It is then that He dwells with the humble and contrite in heart—and thus attends our church! As I listened, I realized that such an attitude was what the Didachist desired to be inculcated in his readers.

My child, the one speaking to you the **word** of God,
[1] you will remember night and day,
[2] and you will honor him as the Lord,
for where the dominion of the Lord is spoken of,
there is the Lord.
[3] And you will seek every day the presence of the saints
in order that you may find support in their **words** (4:1, 2)

Become long-suffering
and merciful
and harmless
and gentle
and good
and one who **trembles** always at the **words**
that you have heard (3:8).

Perhaps amidst all the pressures for churches to adopt the latest fad of worship or of church growth methods, that simple yet powerful message needs to be heard and heeded in our churches today. We are called to honor and respect the one who speaks the word of God in such a way that we tremble in humility and meekness at the word that comes to us through that preacher. No bells and whistles and fancy programs emerge from this—just an attitude of humble obedience that the ancient pagan world found hard to resist. Perhaps that can happen again in the twenty first century!

Appendix One

The Language of the *Didache*

The *Didache* is written in a Hellenistic Greek that is very similar to that of the New Testament. It breathes the spirit of the LXX but with an infusion of Christian meaning in some of the words. It is characterized, like the LXX, by the presence of a number of Hebraisms, but also by the lack of technical, ecclesiastical and dogmatic terms that characterize later patristic writings. The style is simple, natural, terse and sententious.

In these days of computerized texts, it is much easier to do statistical analyses of the vocabulary of a book. I would like to acknowledge, however, the initial statistical work of A.C. McGiffert, who, at the request of Philip Schaff, supplied the following brief statistical breakdown of the vocabulary in the *Didache*. His work was based on the "Jerusalem" manuscript, but the later critical texts have not altered his results in any significant way.

> The *Didache* contains 2,190 words. Its vocabulary comprises 552 words. Of the whole number 504 are New Testament words, 497 are classical, and 479 occur in the LXX. 16 occur for the first time in the *Didache*, but are found in later writers. 1 occurs only in the *Didache* (προεξομολογέομαι, 14.1). 14 occur in the New Testament with a different meaning.[147]

McGiffert and Schaff provide additional tables that illustrate the above statistics which the interested reader can consult. I have chosen not to include them so as not to overburden an already technical appendix. The *Didache* lies open for scholars to perform more advanced types of statistical analyses than McGiffert was able to do. One such labor that has been done by the OpenText.org is an analysis of the entire Greek text book based on their clause analysis methodology. Presently, this work is only available online at opentext.org.

As has been mentioned, of the approximately 552 different words that are in the vocabulary of the Didache, 504 are found in the New Testament. The 48 words that are not in the New Testament are as follows.

Words Not in the New Testament

ἀθάνατος, 4.8, immortal
αἰσχρολόγος, 3.3, foul speech
ἀμφιβολία, 14.2, conflict
ἀνταποδότης, 4.7, paymaster
αὐθάδεια, 5.1, stubbornness
γόγγυσος, 3.6, grumbler
διαφορά, 1.1, difference
διγλωσσία, 2.4, double-tongued
δίγλωσσος, 2.4, double-tongued
διγνώμων, 2.4, double-minded
διπλοκαρδία, 5.1, duplicity
διψυχέω, 4.4, double-minded
εκπέτασις, 16.6, an opening
ἐνδέω, 4.8; 5.2, the one in need
ἐπαοιδός, 3.4, enchanter
ἐριστικός, 3.2, contentious
ζηλοτυπία, 5.1, jealousy
θερμός, 7.2, warm
θράσος, 3.9, boldness
θρασύτης, 5.1, audacity
θυμικός, 3.2, hot-headed
ἱδρόω, 1.6, sweat
κακοήθης, 2.6, spiteful
κοσμοπλανης, 16.4, world-deceiver
κυριακὴ Κυρίου, 14.1, Lord's day of the Lord
μαθηματικός, 3.4, astrologer
μακρόθυμος, 3.8, long-suffering
μῖσος, 16.3, hatred
μνησικακέω, 2.3, to hold a grudge
οἰωνοσκόπος, 3.4, the practice of divination
παιδοφθορέω, 2.2, to corrupt children
πανθαμάρτητος, 5.2, totally sinful
παρόδιος, 12.2, passing through
περικαθαίρω, 3.4, magician
ποθέω, 4.3, to cause
πονέω, 5.2, to work
πονηρόφρων, 3.6, evil-minded

ποτός, 10.3[2x], drink
προνηστεύω, 7.4, to fast
ποροεξομολογέομαι, 14.1, to confess (one's sins) beforehand
πυκνῶς, 16.2, frequently
σιτία, 13.5, bread
συσπάω, 4.5, to draw back
τετράς, 8.1, fourth day
ὑψηλόφθαλμος, 3.3, one who lifts up the eyes
φαρμακεύω, 2.2, to make potions
φθορεύς, 5.2, destroyers; 16.3, corrupters
χριστέμπορος, 12.5, Christ-peddler

In his seminal work on the *Didache*, Bryennios included an abbreviated concordance of its most common words and important phrases.[148] After much deliberation, I have included in this appendix an exhaustive concordance of the words in the *Didache*. Even the most common words are included, but for a few of them I have just mentioned the number of times the word appears without providing the references where they can be found. It is my hope that this concordance will be of value to both students and scholars who desire to dig deeper into the linguistic aspects of the book. My deep gratitude is expressed to my student, Cliff Kvidahl, for his labors in assembling this concordance

Exhaustive Concordance to the Didache

A

ἀγαθός	3.8; 3.10; 5.2[3x]
ἀγαπάω	1.2; 1.3[3x]; 2.7; 5.2[2x]
ἀγάπη	10.5; 16.3
ἀγγαρεύω	1.4
ἁγιάζω	8.2; 10.5
ἅγιος	4.2; 7.1; 7.3; 9.2; 9.5; 10.2[2x]; 10.6; 16.7
ἀγρυπνέω	5.2
ἀδελφός	4.8
ἀθά	10.6
ἀθανασία	10.2
ἀθάνατος	4.8
ἀθέμιτος	16.4
ἀθῷος	1.5[2x]
αἴρω	1.4; 4.9
αἰσχρολογία	5.1
αἰσχρολόγος	3.3
αἰσχύνη	4.11
αἰτέω	1.5; 11.6

αἰών	8.2; 9.2; 9.3; 9.4; 10.2; 10.4; 10.5; 16.4
αἰώνιος	10.3
ἄκακος	3.8
ἀκούω	3.8; 11.2; 11.12; 15.3
ἀλαζονεία	5.1
ἀλήθεια	5.2; 11.10; 16.6
ἀληθής	15.1
ἀληθινός	11.11; 13.1; 13.2
ἀλλά	1.6; 2.5; 2.7; 3.9; 4.9; 4.10; 5.2; 8.2[2x]; 9.5; 11.8; 15.3; 16.1; 16.7
ἀλλήλων	15.3; 16.4
ἄλλος	1.2; 1.4; 7.2; 7.4; 11.2; 11.5; 11.12
ἄλων	13.3
ἁμαρτία	4.6; 11.7[2x]
ἀμήν	10.6
ἄμπελος	9.2
ἀμφιβολία	14.2
ἀμφότεροι	4.10; 7.3
ἄν	1.6; 11.1; 11.12; 13.7
ἀνάγκη	12.2
ἀνάστασις	16.6
ἀναστρέφω	3.9
ἄνεμος	10.5
ἀνήκω	16.2
ἀνήρ	15.1
ἄνθρωπος	2.7; 10.3; 16.5
ἀνοίγω	13.6
ἀνομία	16.4
ἄνομος	5.2
ἀνταπόδομα	5.2
ἀνταποδότης	4.7
ἄξιος	13.1; 13.2; 15.1
ἀπαιτέω	1.4; 1.5
ἀπαρχή	13.3[2x]; 13.5; 13.6; 13.7
ἅπας	3.2; 3.3; 3.4; 3.5; 3.6; 5.2
ἀπέχω	1.4
ἀπό	1.4; 3.1[2x]; 4.9[3x]; 5.2; 6.1; 6.3; 8.2; 9.4; 9.5; 10.5[2x]; 11.8; 11.9; 12.5
ἀποδίδωμι	1.5
ἀποκτείνω	2.2
ἀπόλαυσις	10.3
ἀπόλλυμι	16.5
ἀπόστολος	1.1; 11.3; 11.4; 11.6

ἀποστρέφω	4.8; 5.2
ἀργός	12.4
ἀργύριον	11.6; 11.12; 13.7
ἀρεστός	4.12
ἀριστερός	12.1
ἁρπαγή	5.1
ἅρπαξ	2.6
ἄρτος	8.2; 11.6; 14.1
ἀρχαῖος	11.11
ἀρχιερεύς	13.1
ἀστοχέω	15.3
ἄτερ	3.10
αὐθάδεια	5.1
αὐθάδης	3.6
αὐλίζομαι	11.6
αὐξάνω	16.4
αὐτός	1.3; 1.4[3x]; 3.1; 3.4; 4.1; 4.2; 4.10; 5.2; 8.2; 10.5[4x]; 11.1; 11.2[3x]; 11.9; 11.11; 11.12[2x]; 12.1; 12.2; 13.1; 13.2[2x]; 13.3; 14.2; 15.1; 15.2[2x]; 16.4; 16.5[2x]; 16.7
ἀφαιρέω	4.13
ἀφίημι	8.2[2x]; 11.7[2x]
ἀφιλάργυρος	15.1

B

βαπτίζω	7.1[2x]; 7.2; 7.4[3x]; 9.5
βάπτισμα	7.1; 7.4
βασιλεία	8.2; 9.4; 10.5
βασιλεύς	14.3
βαστάζω	6.2; 6.3
βλασφημία	3.6[2x]
βλέπω	3.4
βοηθέω	12.2
βουλή	2.6
βοῦς	13.3
βρῶσις	6.3

Γ

γάρ	1.3; 1.4; 1.5[3x]; 2.4; 3.2[2x]; 3.3[2x]; 3.4; 3.5; 3.6; 4.1; 4.7; 4.8; 4.10; 6.2; 6.3; 8.1; 9.5; 11.7; 11.11[2x]; 12.1; 13.3; 14.3; 15.1; 15.2; 16.1; 16.2; 16.3; 16.4

γεννάω	2.2; 3.2; 3.3; 3.4; 3.5; 3.6
γέννημα	13.3
γη	3.7; 8.2; 9.4; 16.4
γίνομαι	1.2; 1.5; 3.2; 3.3; 3.4; 3.5; 3.6; 3.8; 3.10; 4.5; 8.2; 9.4; 16.1; 16.4
γινώσκω	1.6; 4.7; 5.2[2x]; 11.8; 12.1
γνωρίζω	9.2; 9.3; 10.2
γνῶσις	9.3; 10.2; 11.2
γογγύζω	4.7
γόγγυσος	3.6
γρηγορέω	16.1

Δ

δαυείδ	9.2; 10.6
δε	(Occurs in 55 verses 70 times)
δεξιός	1.4; 12.1
δεσπότης	10.3
δεύτερος	1.2; 2.1; 8.1
δέχομαι	11.1; 11.2; 11.4; 12.1
διά	1.1; 3.8; 4.6; 9.2; 9.3; 9.4; 10.2; 10.3
διάκονος	15.1
διακρίνω	11.7
διαλλάσσομαι	14.2
διασκορπίζω	9.4
διαφορά	1.1
διγλωσσία	2.4
δίγλωσσος	2.4
διγνώμων	2.4
διδάσκαλος	13.2; 15.1; 15.2
διδάσκω	4.9; 6.1; 11.1; 11.2[2x]; 11.10[2x]; 11.11
διδαχή	1.1; 1.3; 2.1; 6.1; 11.2
δίδωμι	1.4[2x]; 1.5[4x]; 1.6; 3.9; 4.5; 4.6; 4.7[2x]; 8.2; 9.5; 10.3; 11.12[2x]; 13.3; 13.4; 13.5; 13.6; 13.7
δίκαιος	3.9; 5.2
δικαιοσύνη	5.2; 11.2
δικαίως	4.3
δίκη	1.5
διπλοκαρδία	5.1
διστάζω	4.7
διψυχέω	4.4
διώκτης	5.2

διώκω	1.3; 5.2; 16.4
δόγμα	11.3
δοκέω	13.7
δοκιμάζω	11.11; 12.1; 15.1
δοκιμασία	16.5
δόλος	5.1
δόξα	8.2; 9.2; 9.3; 9.4; 10.2; 10.4; 10.5
δοῦλος	4.10; 4.11
δύναμαι	1.4; 6.2[3x]; 6.3; 7.2; 7.4; 12.2
δύναμις	8.2; 9.4; 10.5
δυνατός	10.4
δύο	1.1[2x]; 1.4; 7.4; 12.2
δώδεκα	1.1

E

ἐάν	1.2; 1.3; 1.4[4x]; 4.6; 7.2; 7.3; 11.2; 11.5[2x]; 11.6; 11.8; 11.12; 12.2; 13.4; 13.5; 16.2
ἑαυτοῦ	15.1
ἐγκαταλείπω	4.13
ἐγώ	3.1; 3.3; 3.4; 3.5; 3.6; 4.1; 8.2[9x]; 9.2[2x]; 9.3[2x]; 10.2[2x]; 10.3; 11.12; 14.3[2x]; 15.4; 16.1 (The lexeme ἐγώ does not appear in the text.)
ἔθνος	1.1; 1.3; 14.3
εἰ	1.5; 4.8; 6.2[2x]; 7.2; 7.4; 10.6[2x]; 11.5; 11.6; 11.9; 11.10; 12.2[2x]; 12.3; 12.4; 12.5
εἰδωλόθυτος	6.3
εἰδωλολατρία	3.4[2x]; 5.1
εἰμί	(Occurs in 37 verses, 45 times, in 13 forms)
εἰρηνεύω	4.3
εἰρήνη	15.3
εἰς	1.4; 1.5; 1.6; 3.4; 3.5; 3.6; 5.2[2x]; 7.1; 7.2; 7.3[2x]; 8.2[2x]; 9.2; 9.3; 9.4[2x]; 9.5; 10.2; 10.3; 10.4; 10.5[2x]; 11.2[2x]; 11.11; 16.3[2x]; 16.4; 16.5
εἷς	1.1[2x]; 1.4; 7.4; 9.4; 11.5 (The lexeme εἷς does not appear in the text.)
εἰσφέρω	8.2
εἶτα	16.6
ἐκ	1.5; 3.2; 3.3; 3.4; 3.5; 3.6; 16.4
ἐκεῖ	4.1
ἐκεῖθεν	1.5
ἐκζητέω	4.2

ἐκκλησία	4.14; 9.4; 10.5; 11.11
ἐκλύω	16.1
ἐκπέτασις	16.6
ἐκτείνω	4.5
ἐκχέω	7.3
ἔλαιον	13.6
ἐλέγχω	2.7; 4.3; 15.3
ἐλεέω	5.2
ἐλεημοσύνη	1.6; 15.4
ἐλεήμων	3.8
ἐλπίζω	4.10
ἐμπίπλημι	10.1
ἐν	1.5; 2.2; 4.8[2x]; 4.10; 4.11; 4.14[2x]; 7.1; 7.2[2x]; 8.2[3x]; 10.2; 10.5; 11.7; 11.8; 11.9; 11.12; 12.1; 14.3[2x]; 15.3[3x]; 15.4; 16.1; 16.2; 16.3; 16.5; 16.6
ἐνδέω	4.8; 5.2
ἕνεκα	10.3
ἐνέργημα	3.10
ἐντολή	1.5; 2.1; 4.13; 13.5; 13.7
ἐξέρχομαι	1.5; 11.6
ἐξετάζω	1.5
ἐξομολογέω	4.14
ἐπαναπαύομαι	4.2
ἐπάνω	9.4; 16.8
ἐπαοιδός	3.4
ἐπεί	3.7; 6.1
ἐπειδή	3.4; 3.5; 3.6
ἔπειτα	12.1
ἐπί	4.3; 4.10[3x]; 4.14; 5.2; 8.2; 11.11
ἐπιθυμέω	2.2
ἐπιθυμητής	3.3
ἐπιθυμία	1.4; 3.3; 5.1
ἐπιορκέω	2.3
ἐπιούσιος	8.2
ἐπίσκοπος	15.1
ἐπιτάσσω	4.10
ἐπιτρέπω	10.7
ἐργάζομαι	12.3
ἐργάτης	13.2
ἐριστικός	3.2
ἔρχομαι	4.10; 8.2; 10.6[2x]; 11.1; 11.4; 12.1; 12.2; 16.1, 8
ἐσθίω	9.5; 11.9; 12.3
ἔσχατος	1.5; 16.2; 16.3

ἑταῖρος	14.2
ἕτερος	11.12; 15.3
ἑτοιμάζω	4.19; 10.5
ἕτοιμος	16.1
εὐαγγέλιον	8.2; 11.3; 15.3; 15.4
εὐλογέω	1.3
εὐχαριστέω	9.1; 9.2; 9.3; 10.1; 10.2; 10.3; 10.4; 10.7; 14.1
εὐχαριστία	9.1; 9.5
εὐχή	15.4
ἐχθρός	1.3[2x]
ἔχω	1.3; 1.5[2x]; 4.6; 7.2; 7.3; 11.8; 11.11; 12.1; 12.4; 13.4; 14.215.3; 15.4
ἕως	11.6; 14.2; 15.3

Ζ

ζάω	7.1; 7.2
ζηλοτυπία	5.1
ζηλωτής	3.2
ζητέω	16.2
ζυγός	6.2
ζωή	1.1; 1.2; 4.14; 9.3; 10.3; 16.1

Η

ἤ	4.4; 4.9; 4.10; 7.4; 11.12; 12.2; 13.6
ἥκω	16.5; 16.7
ἡμέρα	4.1; 4.2; 8.3; 11.5; 12.2; 16.3
ἡσύχιος	3.8

Θ

θάνατος	1.1; 2.4; 5.1
θαυμαστός	14.3
θέλημα	8.2
θέλω	1.2; 1.5; 3.4; 10.7; 12.3; 12.5; 13.1
θεός	1.2; 3.10; 4.1; 4.9; 4.10[2x]; 4.11; 5.2; 6.1; 6.3; 10.6; 11.11; 16.4
θερμός	7.2
θλίβω	5.2
θνητός	4.8

θράσος	3.9
θρασύτης	5.1
θυγάτηρ	4.9
θυμικός	3.2
θυσία	14.1; 14.2; 14.3

Ι

ἴδιος	1.5; 4.8
ἱδρόω	1.6
ἰησοῦς	9.2; 9.3; 9.4; 10.2
ἱμάτιον	1.4
ἱματισμός	13.7
ἵνα	4.2; 10.3; 14.2
ἱνατί	1.5

Κ

καθαρός	14.1; 14.3
κάθημαι	12.3; 13.1
καί	(Occurs 97 times)
καιρός	16.2
κακία	5.1
κακοήθης	2.6
κακολογέω	2.3
καλέω	4.10
καλός	4.7
καρδία	10.2
κατά	1.5; 2.6; 4.2; 4.10; 11.3; 12.4; 13.5; 13.7; 14.1; 15.3
κατάθεμα	16.5
καταλύω	11.2
καταπονέω	5.2[2x]
κατάρα	5.1
καταράομαι	1.3
κατασκηνόω	10.2
κελεύω	7.4; 8.2
κενόδοξος	3.5
κενός	2.5
κεράμιον	13.6
κεφαλή	7.3
κλάσμα	9.3; 9.4
κλάω	14.1

κλέπτω	2.2
κληρονομέω	3.7
κλοπή	3.5[2x]; 5.1
κοδράντης	1.5
κοινόω	14.2
κοινωνός	4.8
κολλάω	3.9; 5.2
κοσμικός	11.11
κοσμοπλανής	16.4
κόσμος	10.6; 16.8
κρίνω	4.3; 11.11; 11.12
κρίσις	5.2; 11.11
κριτής	5.2
κτῆμα	13.7
κτίζω	10.3
κτίσις	16.5
κυριακός	14.1
κύριος	1.1; 4.1[2x]; 4.11; 4.12; 4.13; 6.2; 8.2; 9.5[2x]; 10.5; 11.2[2x]; 11.4; 11.8; 12.1; 14.1, 3[2x]; 15.1; 15.4; 16.1; 16.7,8
κυριότης	4.1
κύων	9.5

Λ

λαλέω	4.1[2x]; 11.7; 11.8; 15.3
λαμβάνω	1.4; 1.5[3x]; 2.6; 4.3; 4.5; 11.6; 13.3; 13.5; 13.6, 7
λατρεία	6.3
λέγω	1.6; 4.8; 9.5; 11.12[2x]; 14.3[2x]; 16.7
λειτουργέω	15.1
λειτουργία	15.1
ληνός	13.3
λίαν	6.3
λόγος	1.3; 2.5; 3.8; 4.1; 4.2
λύκος	16.3
λύτρωσις	4.6
λύχνος	16.1

Μ

μαγεία	5.1
μαγεύω	2.2

μαθηματικός	3.4
μακάριος	1.5
μακρόθυμος	3.8
μακρός	5.2
μᾶλλον	4.8
μαράν	10.6
μάταιος	5.2
μάχομαι	4.3
μέγας	14.3
μέν	1.2; 1.5; 2.7; 4.5; 6.2; 12.2
μένω	11.5[2x]; 12.2
μεστός	5.1
μεστόω	2.5
μετά	1.4; 3.9[2x]; 8.1; 10.1; 11.11; 12.4; 14.2; 15.2; 16.7
μετανοέω	10.6; 15.3
μεταξύ	1.1
μέχρι	1.5; 1.6
μή	(Occurs in 34 verses 30 times)
μήγε	11.9
μηδέ	3.2[3x]; 3.3[2x]; 3.4[4x]; 3.5[2x]; 3.6[2x]; 8.2; 9.5; 15.3
μηδείς	9.5; 11.6; 11.12; 15.3
μήποτε	4.10
μήτε	4.13[2x]
μίλιον	1.4
μιμνήσκομαι	4.1; 10.5
μισέω	1.3; 2.7; 4.12; 5.2; 16.4
μισθός	4.7; 5.2
μῖσος	16.3
μνησικακέω	2.3
μοιχεία	3.3; 5.1
μοιχεύω	2.2
μυστήριον	11.11

<u>N</u>

νεκρός	6.3; 16.6
νεότης	4.9
νεφέλη	16.8
νηστεία	8.1
νηστεύω	1.3; 7.4; 8.1[2x]
νύξ	4.1

Ο

ὁ	(Occurs in 90 verses, 270 times, in 24 forms)
ὁδηγέω	3.2; 3.3; 3.4; 3.5; 3.6
ὁδός	1.1[2x]; 1.2; 4.14; 5.1; 6.1
ὅθεν	4.1
οἶδα	3.10; 16.1
οἶνος	13.6
οἰωνοσκόπος	3.4
ὅλος	6.2
ὅμοιος	3.1
ὄνομα	7.1; 7.3; 8.2; 9.5; 10.2; 10.3; 12.1; 14.3
ὅπως	14.1
ὁράω	6.1; 16.8
ὀργή	3.2; 15.3
ὀργίλος	3.2
ὁρίζω	11.9
ὅρος	9.4
ὅς	1.5[2x]; 2.7[3x]; 3.8; 4.10; 4.12; 4.13; 5.2; 6.2; 6.3; 9.2; 9.3; 10.2[2x]; 10.5; 11.1; 11.6; 11.10; 11.12; 14.2; 15.3; 16.1; 16.4
ὅσος	1.2; 10.7; 11.11; 12.2
ὀσφύς	16.1
ὅτι	3.10; 8.2; 9.4; 10.4; 10.5; 14.3
οὐ	(Occurs in 34 verses 59 times)
οὐαι	1.5
οὐδέ	1.4; 2.2; 2.4; 2.6[4x]; 3.9; 4.7; 5.2; 11.7
οὐδείς	3.10
οὐδέποτε	16.4
οὖν	1.2; 11.1; 11.8; 13.3; 15.1; 15.2
οὐρανός	8.2[2x]; 16.6; 16.8
οὗτος	1.2; 1.3[2x]; 1.6; 3.2; 3.3; 3.4; 3.5; 3.6; 4.14; 5.1; 5.2; 6.1; 6.2; 7.1; 9.4; 9.5; 10.6; 11.1; 11.7; 14.3
οὕτω	7.1; 8.2; 8.3; 9.1; 9.4; 10.1; 11.3; 12.5; 15.4
οὐχί	1.3
ὀφειλέτης	8.2
ὀφειλή	8.2

Π

παγίς	2.4
παιδίσκη	4.10

παιδοφθορέω	2.2
παῖς	9.2[2x]; 9.3; 10.2; 10.3
πανθαμάρτητος	5.2
παντοκράτωρ	10.3
παρά	15.3
παραδίδωμι	16.4[2x]
παράκλητος	5.2
παραλαμβάνω	4.13
παράπτωμα	4.3; 4.14; 14.1
παρασκευή	8.1
παρεκτός	6.1
παρέρχομαι	10.6
παρόδιος	12.2
πᾶς	1.2; 1.5[2x]; 2.7; 3.1[2x]; 3.8; 4.8; 4.12[2x]; 5.1; 7.1; 10.3; 10.4; 10.5; 11.1; 11.4; 11.7[2x]; 11.8; 11.9; 11.10; 11.11; 12.1; 13.1; 13.3; 13.7; 14.2; 14.3; 15.3; 15.4; 16.2; 16.7[2x]
πατήρ	1.5; 8.2; 9.2; 9.3; 10.2
πατρήρ	7.1; 7.3
πειράζω	11.7
πειρασμός	8.2
πέμπτος	8.1
πένης	5.2
πέρας	9.4
περί	1.5; 1.6; 2.7; 6.3; 7.1; 9.1; 9.2; 9.3; 9.5; 11.3; 11.12
περὶ δὲ	2.7; 6.3; 7.1; 9.1; 9.3; 11.3
περικαθαίρω	3.4
πικρία	4.10
πίνω	9.5
πίστις	10.2; 16.2; 16.5
πλανάω	6.1
πλάσμα	5.2
πλεονέκτης	2.6
πλεονεξία	5.1
πληθύνω	16.3
πλησίον	1.2; 2.2; 2.6
πλούσιος	5.2
πνεῦμα	4.10; 7.1; 7.3; 11.7; 11.8; 11.9; 11.12
πνευματικός	10.3
ποθέω	4.3
ποιέω	1.2[2x]; 1.3; 5.2; 6.2; 11.3; 11.10; 11.11[4x]; 12.5; 13.5; 15.4
ποίησις	16.4[2x]

ποῖος	1.3
πολύς	1.1; 16.5
πονέω	5.2
πονηρός	2.6; 3.1; 4.14; 5.1; 5.2; 8.2; 10.5
πονηρόφρων	3.6
πορνεία	3.3; 5.1
πορνεύω	2.2
πόσος	4.8
πότερον	4.4
ποτήριον	9.2
ποτός	10.3[2x]
πρᾶξις	2.5; 15.4
πράσσω	1.5
πραΰς	3.7[2x]; 15.1
πραΰτης	5.2
πρό	7.4[2x]; 10.4
πρόβατον	13.3; 16.3
προεξομολογέομαι	14.1
προλέγω	7.1; 11.1
προνηστεύω	7.4
προνοέω	12.4
πρός	3.2; 3.3; 4.5[2x]; 11.4; 12.2; 12.3; 13.1
προσδέχομαι	3.10
προσέρχομαι	4.14
προσευχή	4.14
προσεύχομαι	1.3; 2.7; 8.2[2x]; 8.3
προσέχω	6.3; 12.5
προστίθημι	4.13; 11.2
προσφέρω	14.3
πρόσωπον	4.2; 4.3; 4.10
προφήτης	10.7; 11.3; 11.7; 11.8[2x]; 11.9; 11.10; 11.11[2x]; 13.1; 13.3; 13.4; 13.6; 15.1; 15.2
πρῶτος	1.2; 5.1; 9.2; 16.6
πτωχός	5.2; 13.4
πυκνῶς	16.2
πύρωσις	16.5
πῶς	12.4

Ρ

ῥάπισμα	1.4
ῥύομαι	5.2; 8.2; 10.5

Σ

σάββατον	8.1
σάλπιγξ	16.6
σαρκικός	1.4
σβέννυμι	16.1
σεαυτοῦ	1.2; 3.9
σημεῖον	16.4; 16.6[3x]
σήμερον	8.2
σιαγών	1.4
σιτία	13.5
σκανδαλίζω	16.5
σός	1.4; 9.4; 10.5
στρέφω	1.4; 11.2; 16.3[2x]
σύ	(Occurs in 45 verses, 91 times, in 9 forms)
συγκοινωνέω	4.8
συμβαίνω	3.10
συνάγω	9.4[2x]; 10.5; 14.1; 16.2
συνείδησις	4.14
συνέρχομαι	14.2
σύνεσις	12.2; 12.4
συνοχή	1.5
συσπάω	4.5
σχίσμα	4.3
σώζω	16.5
σωματικός	1.4

Τ

ταπεινός	3.9
τε	10.3; 13.3
τέκνον	2.2; 3.1; 3.3; 3.4; 3.5; 3.6; 4.1; 5.2[2x]
τέλειος	1.4; 6.2
τελειόω	10.5; 16.2
τέρας	16.4
τέσσαρες	10.5
τετράς	8.1
τέχνη	12.4
τεχνίτης	12.3
τιμάω	4.1; 15.2
τὶς	1.4[4x]; 1.5[2x]; 1.6; 4.7; 6.1; 7.4; 10.6[2x]; 11.12

τοιοῦτος	12.5
τόπος	14.3
τότε	16.4; 16.5; 16.6; 16.8
τράπεζα	11.9
τρεῖς	7.3; 8.3; 11.5; 12.2
τρέμω	3.8
τρίτος	16.6
τρόπος	11.8[2x]
τροφή	10.3[2x]; 13.1; 13.2
τύπος	4.11

Υ

ὕδωρ	7.1; 7.2[2x]; 7.3
υἱός	4.9; 7.1; 7.3; 16.4
ὑπάγω	1.4
ὑπέρ	1.3[2x]; 2.7; 9.2; 9.3; 10.2[2x]; 16.1
ὑπερηφανία	5.1
ὑπερήφανος	2.6
ὑπεροράω	15.2
ὑπό	14.3; 16.5
ὑπόκρισις	4.12; 5.1
ὑποκριτής	2.6; 8.1; 8.2
ὑπομένω	16.5
ὑπομονή	5.2
ὑποτάσσω	4.11
ὑστερέω	11.12
ὑψηλός	3.9
ὑψηλόφθαλμος	3.3
ὕψος	5.1
ὑψόω	3.9

Φ

φαίνω	16.4; 16.6
φαρμακεία	5.1
φαρμακεύω	2.2
φεύγω	3.1
φθορά	2.2
φθορεύς	5.2; 16.3
φιλάργυρος	3.5
φοβέω	4.10
φόβος	4.9; 4.11

φονεύς   5.2
φονεύω   2.2[2x]
φόνος   3.2[2x]; 5.1
φυλάσσω   4.13
φωνή   16.6

X

χαρίζομαι   10.3
χάρις   1.3; 10.6
χάρισμα   1.5
χείρ   1.6; 4.5; 4.6; 4.9; 16.4
χειροτονέω   15.1
χιτών   1.4
χρεία   1.5[2x]; 11.5
χριστέμπορος   12.5
χριστιανός   12.4
χριστός   9.4
χρόνος   14.3; 16.2

Ψ

ψευδής   2.5
ψευδομαρτυρέω   2.3
ψευδομαρτυρία   5.1
ψευδοπροφήτης   11.5; 11.6; 11.8; 11.9; 11.1o; 16.3
ψεῦδος   5.2
ψεῦσμα   3.5
ψεύστης   3.5
ψυχή   2.7; 3.9[2x]; 16.2
ψυχρός   7.2

Ω

ὥρα   16.1
ὡς   1.2; 3.10; 4.1; 4.11; 8.2[4x]; 11.2; 11.4; 13.7; 15.3; 15.4;
                 16.4; 16.7
ὡσαννά   10.6
ὡσαύτως   11.11; 13.2; 13.6
ὥσπερ   9.4; 13.2
ὠφελέω   16.2

Appendix Two

Topical Index to the *Didache*

In the previous index, we provided a concordance of all the Greek words in the *Didache*. That may not be helpful, however, for the person who simply would like to study the *Didache* apart from any knowledge of Greek. Therefore, this appendix consists of an index to all the topics found in the book. I would like to thank my former student, Abner Chou, for compiling this index.

Endnotes

CHAPTER ONE: Introduction to the *Didache*

1. William Varner, "The *Didache*'s Use of the Old and New Testaments" *The Masters Seminary Journal*, Volume 16, Number 1 (Spring, 2005): 127-51; "What the *Teaching* Can Teach Us" *Christianity Today* Volume 50, Number 6 (2006): 30-32.

2. Joan Hazelden Walker, "Reflections on a new Edition of the *Didache*," *Vigiliae Christianae* 35 (1981): 35.

3. Kurt Niederwimmer, *The Didache*, (Minneapolis: Fortress Press, 1998); Aaron Milavec, *The Didache: Faith, Hope and Life of the Earliest Christian Communities, 50-70 C.E.*, (New York: Newman Press, 2003).

4. *The Didache in Context: Essays on its Text, History and Transmission*, ed. Clayton Jefford, (New York: E.J. Brill, 1995); *The Didache in Modern Research*, ed. Jonathan A. Draper, (New York: E.J. Brill, 1996); and *The Didache: Its Jewish Sources and Its Place in Early Judaism and Christianity*, eds. Huub van de Sandt and David Flusser, (Minneapolis: Fortress Press, 2002); *Matthew and the Didache: Two Documents from the Same Jewish-Christian Milieu?*, ed. Huub van de Sandt, (Minneapolis: Fortress Press, 2005).

5. See as a recent sample, Jonathan Draper, "Ritual Process and Ritual Symbol in *Didache* 7-10" *Vigiliae Christianae* 54, 2 (2000): 121-158; Clayton Jefford, "Conflict at Antioch: Ignatius and the *Didache* at Odds" *Studia Patristica* 36 (2001): 262-269; Huub van de Sandt, "Do not give what is holy to the dogs (Did. 9:5d and Matt. 7:6a; the Eucharistic food of the *Didache* in its Jewish Purity Setting" Vigiliae *Christianae* 56, 3 (2002): 223-246; and Jonathan Draper, "The Apostolic Fathers: The *Didache*" *The Expository Times* 117, 5 (2006): 177-81.

6. "The New Testament and the Apostolic Fathers," Oxford University, April 5-7, 2004. The conference was called to commemorate the 100th anniversary of the publication of a seminal volume titled *The New Testament in the Apostolic Fathers* produced in 1905 by the Oxford Committee on Historical Theology. The proceedings have been published as *The New Testament and the Apostolic Fathers*, eds. Andrew Gregory and Christopher Tuckett, (Oxford: Oxford University Press, 2006), 2 volumes.

7. See e.g., David Flusser, footnote 4 and the early article by Kaufmann Kohler in the *Jewish Encyclopedia,* Isidore Singer, ed. (New York: Ktav Publishing House, 1901): IV, 585-88.

8. See the following standard works for treatments of these important "introductory" issues: J.B. Lightfoot, *The Apostolic Fathers* (London: Macmillan, 1893), 2nd edition, ed.

Michael Holmes (Grand Rapids: Baker, 1999); Niederwimmer, chapters 1-7; and Milavec, Parts 1 and 2.

9. This is the general position of the contributors to *Matthew and the Didache.* (2005). See also the recent article by Jonathan Draper, "The Apostolic Fathers: The *Didache*," (2006).

10. See, e.g., Milavec, vii-xxv. As early as 1885 the French scholar Sabatier defended this early date (*La Didache.* Paris: Librairie Fischbacher). Jean Paul Audet in *La Didache: Instruction des Apotres* (Paris: Librairie Lecoffre, 1958) has provided the most scholarly defense of a very early date, although he does acknowledge a number of later editorial additions to the document.

11. Stephen Neill and NT Wright, *The Interpretation of the New Testament, 1861-1986* (Oxford: Oxford University Press, 1988), 2nd ed., 64.

12. See, e.g., the commentary by Niederwimmer; Willy Rordorf and Andre Tuilier, *La doctrine des douze apôtres.* 1978 edition republished and enlarged (Paris: Cerf, 1998), and Alan Garrow, *The Gospel of Matthew's Dependence on the Didache* (London, New York: TandT Clark, 2004).

13. Those influential writers will be discussed in later chapters where their contributions to the discussion of various issues will be noted.

CHAPTER TWO: The Rediscovery of the *Didache*
14. Two of the scholars on the list were David Flusser, who reported on his own examination of the manuscript in *The Didache*, 16-24, and Willy Rordorf, another major *Didache* scholar. I did not recognize the name of the third "reader" who signed the sheet. There surely have been more than these who have visited the library to see the *Didache.* For example, the Notre Dame scholar, David Aune, informed me in a private email that he had also examined the manuscript in Jerusalem in 2002.

15. Philotheos Bryennios, Διδαχη Των Δωδεκα Αποστολων (Constantinople: Tupois S.I. Voutyra, 1883).

16. Recent scholars have seriously questioned the romantic version of the scroll's discovery, although Muhammad ed Dihb and his relatives never abandoned their original account of the scroll's "accidental" discovery. See Hershel Shanks, editor, *Understanding the Dead Sea Scrolls* (New York: Random House, 1992).

17. Edwin A Grosvenor, "An Interview with Bishop Bryennios-The Discovery of the Teaching," *Andover Review* November (1884): 515-16.

18. Philotheos Bryennios, Του εν αγιοις πατρος ημων Κλεμεντος επισκοπου Ρωμης αι δυο προς Κορινθιους επιστολαι (Constantinople, 1875).

19. See the discussion of the Alexandrinus "Clements" by J.B. Lightfoot, *Apostolic Fathers*, vol. 1, (Grand Rapids: Baker Book House, 1981 reprint of the original 1890 edition.): 116-21.

20. J. Rendel Harris, *The Teaching of the Apostles* (Baltimore: Johns Hopkins, 1887). The ten photographic plates follow page 107.

21. Bryennios, κ' (20).

22. Adolf Harnack, *Die Lehre der Zwölf Apostel: Texte und Untersuchungen zur Geschichte der Altchristlichen Literatur.* Vol. 2 (Leipzig: Hinrichs, 1886): 1-70, and "Didache," in *The New Schaff-Herzog Encyclopedia of Religious Knowledge* S.M. Jackson, ed. New York: Funk & Wagnalls, 1906: III, 420-24. Harnack also assigned the verse

divisions which have been used until today. Bryennios had earlier divided the work into its sixteen chapters.

23. Schaff, 12, 121.

24. See the discussion, e.g., in J.E.L. Oulton, "Clement of Alexandria and the *Didache*" *JTS* 41 (1940): 177-79.

25. Bart Ehrman, "The New Testament Canon of Didymus the Blind" *Vigiliae Christianae* Volume 37, no. 1 (March, 1983): 11-13, 16-17, 21.

26. Van de Sandt and Flusser, 112-39.

27. Bernard Grenfell and Arthur Hunt, *Oxyrhynchus Papyri*, Part XV. (London: Egypt Exploration Society, 1922): 12-15.

28. See Varner (2006) for accompanying photos of the fragment.

29. Colin Roberts, *Manuscript, Society and Belief in Early Christian Egypt* (London: Oxford, 1979): 10-15.

30. G.W.H. Lampe, *A Patristic Greek Lexicon* (Oxford: Oxford University Press, 1981): 405.

31. Markus Bockmuehl, *Seeing the Word: Refocusing New Testament Study* (Grand Rapids: Baker Academic, 2006): 64-68.

CHAPTER THREE: The Text of the *Didache*

32. Grenfell and Hunt, 12-15.

33. Bryennios, 37.

34. Harris, 1-10.

35. Karl Bihlmeyer, *Die Apostolischen Vater: Neubearbeitung Der Funkschen Ausgabe*, Ester Teil (Tubingen: J.C.B. Mohr, 1970), 1-9.

36. Klaus Wengst, *Didache, Barnabasbrief, Zweiter Clementsbrief, Schrift an Diognet* (Munchen: Kosel-Verlag, 1984), 66-91.

37. Willy Rordorf and Andrew Tuilier, *La doctrine des douze apôtres*. 1978 edition republished with extended bibliography and notes as part of the *Sources Christienns* series (Paris: Cerf, 1998), 142-99.

38. Both Rordorf/Tuilier and Bihlmeyer add these bracketed words that appear in the *Doctrina Apostolorum* and the *Apostolic Church Order*.

39. Rordorf/Tuilier and Bihlmeyer add this word due to its inclusion in the *Doctrina Apostolorum*, *Barnabas*, and *Apostolic Constitutions*.

40. The inclusion of the name Iησοῦ is attested only in the Coptic version. Although a case can be made for its inclusion due to the parallels in the previous verses, it is best to not include it due to its late attestation.

41. The Coptic version and the *Apostolic Constitutions* include, with some variations, an interesting prayer over "ointment" (μύρου). It is not included due to its late attestation and to the fact that it is nowhere recorded that Jesus ever made known the "ointment" as he did the other blessings in 9:2,3 and 10:2,3.

42. The words are found in a similar sentence at 12.2, are supported by the Ethiopic version, and make better sense in the context. The inclusion of the name Iησοῦ is attested only in the Coptic version. Although a case can be made for its inclusion due to the parallels in the previous verses, it is best to not include it due to its late attestation.

CHAPTER FOUR: A Translation of the *Didache*
43. Milavec, *The Didache*, 2003: 9-45.
44. Aelred Cody, "The *Didache*: An English Translation," in *The Didache in Context: Essays on Its Text, History, & Transmission*, ed. by Clayton Jefford (Leiden: E.J. Brill, 1995), 3-14.

CHAPTER FIVE: The Scriptures of the *Didache*
45. The literature in this area is extensive and continues to expand. For three recent works that illustrate various approaches to the hermeneutical implications of the "Old in the New," see Greg Beale, ed., *The Right Doctrine from the Wrong Texts?* (Grand Rapids: Baker Books, 1994); Steve Moyise, *The Old Testament in the New* (New York: Continuum, 2001); and Craig Evans, ed., *From Prophecy to Testament: The Function of the Old Testament in the New* (Peabody, MA: Hendrickson Publishers, 2004).
46. David E. Aune, *The Westminster Dictionary of New Testament and Early Christian Literature and Rhetoric* (Louisville: Westminster John Knox Press, 2003) 395.
47. A sampling of Patristic authors through the fourth century who utilized this Malachi text as prophetic of the eucharist in the same way as the Didachist include Justin Matryr, *Dialogue with Trypho* 41:2; 116.3; 117:1,4; Clement of Alexandria, *Stromata* 5.136.2,3; Irenaeus *Heresies* 4.17.5,6; and Tertullian, *Adversus Judaeos* 5.4; 5.7; *Against Marcion* 3.22.6; 4.1.8; Lactantius, *Divine Institutions* 4.11.8; Origen, *Homily on Genesis*, 13.3; Eusebius, *Demonstratio* 1,10,35; 3,2,74; and Cyril of Alexandria, *Catechesis ad Illuminados* A 18,25.
48. George Eldon Ladd, "The Eschatology of the *Didache*" (Harvard University, 1949), 145-155.
49. For a creative suggestion about the content of that missing ending, see Robert Aldridge, "The Lost Ending of the *Didache*," *Vigiliae Christianae*, 53: 1-15.
50. Some see another possible allusion to Luke 12:35 in *Didache* 16:1a.
51. See, for example, Schaff, 78-88. Schaff also believed that the *Didache* showed implicit knowledge of some other NT books, a position not often advocated by scholars today, 88-95.
52. Edouard Massaux, *The Influence of the Gospel of Saint Matthew on Christian Literature before Saint Irenaeus* Book 3: "The Apologists and the *Didache*." English translation ed. by Arthur Bellinzoni (Macon: Mercer University Press, 1993).
53. Helmut Koester, *Synoptische Uberlieferung bei den apostolischen Vatern*. TU, vol. 65 (Berlin: Akademie-Verlag, 1957).
54. See, for example, Jonathan Draper, "The Jesus Tradition in the *Didache*" in *Gospel Perspectives*, vol. 5, *The Jesus Tradition Outside the Gospels*, ed. David Wenham (Sheffield: JSOT, 1985) 269-287. Papers at the "New Testament and the Apostolic Fathers" conference in 2004 presented by Arthur Bellinzoni, William Peterson and Helmut Koester still advocated this position. This is also the general position of most of the authors in *Matthew and the Didache*.
55. Jean Paul Audet, *La Didache Instructions des Apotres* (Paris: Librarie Lecoffre, 1958). See endnotes 10, 11.
56. Christopher Tuckett, "Synoptic Tradition in the *Didache*" in *The Didache in Modern Research*, ed. Jonathan Draper (Leiden: EJ Brill, 1996), 92-128.
57. Udo Schnelle, *The History and Theology of the New Testament Writings* (Minneapolis: Fortress Press, 1998), 355.

58. Martin Hengel, *The Four Gospels and the One Gospel of Jesus Christ* (Harrisburg: Trinity Press, 2000), 64.

59. Tuckett, 128,129.

60. Bruce Metzger, *The Text of the New Testament* (New York: Oxford University Press, 1968) 87.

61. This is much like Paul's use of the very same discourse marker to introduce the successive subjects he was addressing in his First Epistle to the Corinthians (7:1; 7:25; 8:1; 12:1; 16:1; 16:12).

62. Oskar Skarsaune, *In the Shadow of the Temple: Jewish Influences on Early Christianity*, (Downers Grove, IL: Inter Varsity Press, 2002) 406-421.

63. Draper, "Jesus Tradition in the *Didache*," 78.

64. W.D. Davies and D.C. Allison, *Matthew 1-7* (London: T&T Clark, 1988), 676; and D.A Carson, "Matthew" in *Expositors Bible Commentary*, vol. 8 (Grand Rapids: Zondervan, 1984) 185.

65. Andre Tuilier, "La *Didache* at le probleme synoptique," in Jefford, *The D idache in Context*, 110-130 ; and "Les charismatiques itinerants dans la Didache et dans l'Evangile de Matthieu (with an English abstract)" in Van de Sandt, *Matthew and the Didache*: 157-72.

66. Lampe, 549.

67. Tuilier, "La *Didache*," 130.

68. Patrick Skehan, "*Didache* 1, 6 and Sirach 12, 1" *Biblica* 44, 1963, 533-536.

69. Bryennios, 56. Robert M. Grant mentions the use of *Sirach* also at 4:8 (*Sir.* 4:5); 4:5 (*Sir.* 4:36); 1:2 (*Sir.* 7:30); 13:3 (*Sir.* 7:31-32); and 1:4 (*Sir.* 8:1). *Apostolic Fathers* (New York: Nelson, 1964), Vol. 1, 75n. Comparative examination of these texts indicates more a level of *echo* rather than of *citation*.

CHAPTER SIX: The Two Ways of the *Didache*

70. I will only mention a few of the main books and articles on this subject in the last fifty years. Jean Paul Audet in *La Didache: Instruction des Apotres* (Paris: 1958); Jean Danielou, *The Theology of Jewish Christianity I* (London: Darton, Longman and Todd, 1964) 28ff., 315ff.;   Jean-Paul Audet, "Literary and Doctrinal Affinities of the Manual of Discipline" in Draper, *Didache*, 129-147.

71. *Matthew and the Didache: Two Documents from the Same Jewish-Christian Milieu?*, ed. Huub van de Sandt, (Minneapolis: Fortress Press, 2005), 238-70.

72. Jean-Paul Audet, "Literary and Doctrinal Affinities of the Manual of Discipline" in Draper, *Didache*, 129-147.

73. Willy Rordorf, "An Aspect of the Judaeo-Christian Ethic: The Two Ways" in Draper *The Didache*, 151.

74. B.B. Warfield, "Notes on the *Didache*" *Journal of the Exegetical Society, June*, 1886, 92-93.

75. For the text in English, see Geza Vermes, *The Complete Dead Sea Scrolls in English* (Penguin, 1997) 101-103. For a brief summary discussion of the rabbinic concept of the two inclinations in man, see Jacob Neusner, ed. *Dictionary of Judaism in the Biblical Period* (New York: Simon and Schuster) 312, 668.

76. Wilhelm Michaelis, "ὁδός," in *Theological Dictionary of the New Testament*, (Grand Rapids: Eerdmans Publishing, 1967), Volume V, 53-60, 93-96.

77. Aaron Milavec, *The Didache: Faith, Hope and Life of the Earliest Christian Communities, 50-70 C.E.*, (New York: Newman Press, 2003).

78. Aaron Milavec, *The Didache: Text, Translation, Analysis, and Commentary* (Collegeville, MN: Liturgical Press, 2003).

79. Milavec, *The Didache: Text*, 44-61.

80. Milavec, *The Didache: Text*, 41.

81. Milavec, *The Didache: Text*, 49-50. As is so often the case, Milavec provides in his longer work more evidence for adopting this interpretation. Milavec, *The Didache: Faith*, 112-16.

82. For considerations of space, I do not always quote in its entirety the *Didache* text to which I am referring. Readers are requested to consult the Analytical Translation in chapter four, pages 29-42.

83. Daniel B. Wallace, *Greek Grammar Beyond the Basics: An Exegetical Syntax of the New Testament* (Grand Rapids: Zonbervan, 1997): 569-70.

84. Milavec, *The Didache: Text*, 53.

85. David N. Freedman, ed. *Anchor Bible Dictionary* (New York: Doubleday, 1992): I, 34.

86. While the translation is mine, I again acknowledge the influence of Aaron Milavec on my utilizing an analytical translation, which he also has pioneered in his own works on the *Didache*.

87. The contemporary Jewish scholar, Jacob Neusner, has eloquently issued this warning in a number of his many valuable volumes.

88. Huub van de Sandt and David Flusser illustrate this Jewish characteristic of 3:1-6 with a wealth of examples from Jewish literature in *The Didache: Its Jewish Sources and its Place in Early Judaism and Christianity*, 165-179 (see endnote 4).

89. Schaff, 93.

90. An excellent review of the recent scholarly discussion on the *Haustafeln* is provided in a thorough excursus by Harold Hoehner, *Ephesians: An Exegetical Commentary* (Grand Rapids: Baker, 2002): 720-29.

91. Milavec, *The Didache: Text*, 60.

CHAPTER SEVEN: The Sacraments of the *Didache*

92. Van de Sandt and Flusser, "A Jewish-Christian Addition to the Two Ways: Did. 6:2, 3": 238-70.

93. David Flusser, "Paul's Jewish-Christian Opponents in the *Didache*," in *The Didache in Modern Research*, ed. Jonathan Draper, 195-211.

94. Niederwimmer, 122-23; Rordorf and Tuilier, 32-33.

95. Willy Rordorf, "Baptism in the Didache," in *The Didache in Modern Research*," ed. Jonathan Draper, 212-22.

96. Rordorf, 221-22.

97. Schaff, 29-35.

98. This lecture is published as "The Apostolic Fathers and Infant Baptism" in *Trajectories through the New Testament and the Apostolic Fathers*, Andrew Gregory and Chistopher Tuckett, eds. (Oxford: Oxford University Press, 2005): 123-33.

99. Abundant examples of such immersion *mikveh* installations have been uncovered in the land of Israel. These *mikvaot* also contain entrances and exits for the water so there would always be "living water" flowing through the *mikveh*.

100. Schaff, 34.

101. See Schaff, 35 for these references.

102. For the various views and an excellent discussion of this passage, see Jonathan A. Draper, "Christian Self-Definition against the "Hypocrites" in *Didache* 8," in Draper, *The Didache in Modern Research*: 223-43.

103. Johannes Betz, "The Eucharist in the Didache" in Jonathan A. Draper, *The Didache in Modern Research*: 245. Betz's thorough discussion of these issues (245-75), along with the following chapter by Enrico Mazza, "Didache 9-10: Elements of a Eucharisic Interpretation" (276-99) offer a most thorough and up-to-date handling of these questions.

104. Willy Rordorf, "The Didache" in *The Eucharist of the Early Christians* (New York: Pueblo Publishing Co., 1976): 1-21. Rordorf also offers additonal valuable insight into these chapters in Rordorf and Tuilier, 38-48, 63-73 (endnote 12).

105. For an able discussion of the Jewish context of these prayers, see Oskar Skarsaune, *In the Shadow of the Temple: Jewish Influences on Early Christanity* (Downers Grove: InterVarsity Press, 2002): 399-421.

106. Rordorf, 6.

107. Audet, 372-98.

108. Skarsaune, 411.

109. Rordorf, 9.

110. Bart Ehrman, translator, *The Apostolic Fathers*, Vol. One, *Loeb Classical Library* (Cambridge: Harvard University Press, 2003), 24: 431-33.

111. Rordorf, 14.

112. Rordorf, 15.

113. Rordorf, 17.

CHAPTER EIGHT: The Ministers of the *Didache*

114. Andre de Halleux has effectively surveyed the different interpretations of these "ministers" and offered his own informed interpretation in "Ministers in the Didache," Jonathan A. Draper, ed. *The Didache in Modern Research*: 300-320. I have generally followed the approach of Simon Tugwell, *The Apostolic Fathers* (Harrisburg, PA: Morehouse Publishing, 1990): 1-5.

115. In the mid-second century, Lucian exposes the philosopher Peregrinus by presenting him as exploiting Christian hospitality. As he wandered, he had "the Christians as sufficient provisions for hs journey" (*De Morte Peregrini*, 16). Cited by Tugwell, 18n.

116. Danker, 1090.

117. Schaff, 125-27.

118. Schaff, 126n.

119. Tugwell, 3.

120. Milavec, 73, for example.

121. Walter Bauer, *A Greek-English Lexicon of the New Testament and other Early Christian Literature*, 3d ed.. Fredrick W. Danker, ed. (Chicago: University of Chicago Press, 2000): 1013.

122. Schaff, 75.

CHAPTER NINE: The Theology of the *Didache*

123. I have refrained from providing references to illustrate this point, since I do not wish to appear that I am attacking writers for their lack of theological acumen.

124. Schaff, 22.

125. One of the earliest efforts in this regard was by the German Catholic scholar Krawutzky in 1884. Schaff duscusses and critically interacts with his views and offers a rejoinder that also applies to the few scholars who later have advanced this charge of Ebionism. See Schaff, 23-24.

126. In this regard the reader is referred to the tendential treatment by Bart Ehrman, *Lost Christianities:The Battles for Scripture and the Faiths We Never Knew* (Oxford: Oxford University Press, 2003): 95-103. For more even handed treatments, there is the long out of print and hard to secure volume by Hugh J. Schonfield, *The History of Jewish Christianity* (London: Duckworth, 1936). The best treatment of the subject is the scholarly volume edited by Oskar Skarsaune and Reidar Hvalvik, *Jewish Believers in Jesus: The Early Centuries* (Peabody, MA: Hendrickson Publishers, 2006).

127. Oscar Cullmann, *The Christology of the New Testament* (Louisville, KY: Westminster John Knox Press, 1980):64-65.

128. Cullmann, 73.

129. Cullmann, 73.

130. Cullmann, 75.

131. Schaff, 26.

132. Thomas F. Torrance, *The Doctrine of Grace in the Apostolic Fathers* (Grand Rapids: Eerdmans publishing Co., 1959): 36-43.

133. Lampe, 786.

134. Schaff, 26.

135. F.F. Bruce, "The Eschatology of the Apostolic Fathers," in *The Heritage of the Early Church* (Rome: Pontificum Institutum Studiorum Orientalium, 1973): 83.

136. See the articles by Milavec and Pardee in Jefford, *The Didache in Context* and the articles by Bammel and Seeliger in Draper, *The Didache In Modern Research.*

137. George Eldon Ladd, "The Eschatology of the Didache," Ph.D. diss., Harvard University, 1949.

138. Hans Reinhard Seeliger, "Considerations on the Background and Purpose of the Apocalyptic Conclusion of the Didache," in Draper, *Didache in Modern Research:* 374-76. It is ironic that Seeliger still refers to the chapter as "apocalyptic" in the title!

139. Seeliger, 374. Collin's definition as given is the result of the work of the Genres Project of the Society of Biblical Literature.

140. Seeliger, 381.

141. Danker, 517; Lampe, 708.

142. Schaff, 215-16. See Nancy Pardee in Jefford, *The Didache in Context:* 156-76, for another thorough evaluation of the verse.

143. Danker, 307, citing Wengst.

144. See Schaff, 218; and Ladd, 33ff. Both believed that the eschatological views of the *Didache* were at least consistent with pre-millennialism.

145. Robert E. Aldridge, "The Lost Ending of the *Didache*" *Vigiliae Christianae* 53 (1999): 1-15.

146. Ladd, 177. I have paraphrased Ladd with my own nuancing at certain points.

CHAPTER TEN: The Lessons of the *Didache*

146 .Milavec, *The Didache: Text:* 88.

147. Schaff, 97.

148. Bryennios, 58-61.

Bibliography

Aland, Kurt. *Did the Early Church Baptize Infants?* London: SCM, 1963.

Aldridge, Robert E. "The Lost Ending of the *Didache.*" *Vigiliae Christianae* 53 (1999): 1-15.

Audet, Jean-Paul. "Literary and Doctrinal Relationships of the 'Manual.'" In *The Didache in Modern Research.* Ed. Jonathan A. Draper. Leiden: E.J. Brill, 1996: 129-47.

————. *La Didache: Les instructions des apôtres.* Paris: J. Gabalda, 1958.

Aune, David E. *Prophesy in Early Christianity and the Ancient Mediterranean World.* Grand Rapids: Eerdmans, 1983.

Bacchiocchi, Samuele. *From Sabbath to Sunday.* Rome: Pontifical Gregorian Univ, 1977.

————. "The Rise of Sunday Observance in Early Christianity." In *The Sabbath in Scripture and History.* Ed. Kenneth A. Strand. Washington, DC: Review and Herald, 1982: 132-50.

Bahr, Gordon J. "The Use of the Lord's Prayer in the Primitive Church." *JBL* 84 (1965): 153-59.

Bammel, Ernst. "Pattern and Prototype of *Didache* 16." In *The Didache in Modern Research.* Ed. Jonathan A. Draper. Leiden: E.J. Brill, 1996: 364-72.

Barnard, L.W. "The Dead Sea Scroll, Barnabas, the *Didache* and the Later History of the 'Two Ways.'" In *Studies in the Apostolic Fathers and Their Background.* Oxford: Basil Blackwell, 1966: 87-109.

Bartlet, J.V. "The *Didache* Reconsidered." *JTS* 22 (1921): 239-49.

————, et al. "The *Didache.*" In *The New Testament in the Apostolic Fathers.* Oxford: Clarendon, 1905: 24-36

Bauer, Walter. *A Greek-English Lexicon of the New Testament and other Early Christian Literature,* 3d ed. Ed. Fredrick W. Danker. Chicago: University of Chicago Press, 2000.

Beckwith, Rodger T. "The Daily and Weekly Worship of the Primitive Church in Relation to its Jewish Antecedents." *Evangelical Quarterly* 56, no. 2 (1984): 65-80.

Betz, O. "Review of Willy Rordorf, *Sunday.*" *JBL* 83 (1964): 81-83.

————. "The Eucharist in the *Didache.*" In *The Didache in Modern Research.* Ed. Jonathan A. Draper. Leiden: E.J. Brill, 1996: 244-75.

Bigg, C. *The Doctrine of the Twelve Apostles.* Translation and notes. London: S.P.C.K., 1922.

Bihlmeyer, Karl. *Die Apostolischen Väter.* Tübigen: Mohr, 1970.

Bradshaw, Paul F. *Daily Prayer in the Early Church: The Study of the Origin and Early Development of the Divine Office.* New York: Oxford University Press, 1982.
———. *The Search for the Origins of Christian Worship.* New York: Oxford University Press, 2002.
Brown, Raymond E. "*Episkopē* and *Episkopos*: The New Testament Evidence." *TS* 22 (1980): 322-38. Reprinted in R. Brown 1981: 96-106.
———. *The Churches the Apostles Left Behind.* New York: Paulist, 1984.
———. and Meier, John P. *Antioch and Rome: New Testament Cradles of Catholic Christianity.* New York: Paulist Press, 1983.
Bruce, F.F. 'The Eschatology of the Apostolic Fathers." In *The Heritage of the Early Church* (Rome: Pontificum Institutum Studiorum Orientalium, 1973): 77-89.
Bryennios, Philotheos., *Διδαχη Των Δωδεκα Αποστολων* (Constantinople: Tupois S.I. Voutyra, 1883).
———. *Του εν αγιοις πατρος ημων Κλεμεντος επισκοπου Ρωμης αι δυο προς Κοριν θιους επιστολαι* (Constantinople, 1875).
Burkitt, G.C. "Barnabas and the *Didache*." *JTS* 33 (1932): 25-27.
Butler, B.C. "The Literary Relations of the *Didache*, Ch. XVI." *JTS* 11 (1960): 265-83.
———. "The Two Ways in the *Didache*." *JTS* 12 (1961): 27-38.
Cadbury, H.J. "Epistle of Barnabas and the *Didache*." *JQR* 26 (1936): 403-6.
Cody, Aelred. "The *Didache*: An English Translation." In *The Didache in Context: Essays on Its Text, History and Transmission.* Ed. Clayton N. Jefford. Leiden: E.J. Brill, 1995: 3-14.
Connolly, R.H. "Fragments of the *Didache*." *JTS* 25 (1924): 151-53.
———. "The *Didache* in Relations to the Epistle of Barnabas." *JTS* 33 (1932): 237-53.
———. "Agape and Eucharist in the *Didache*." *Downside Review* 55 (1937): 477-89.
———. "Barnabas and the *Didache*." *JTS* 38 (1937): 165-67.
Court, John M. "The *Didache* and St. Matthew's Gospel." *SJT* 34, no. 2 (1981): 109-20.
———. "Right and Left: Implications for Matthew 25:31-46." *NTS* 31 (1985): 223-33.
Creed, J.M. "The *Didache*." *JTS* 39 (1938): 370-87.
Cross, F.L., E.A. Livingstone. *The Oxford Dictionary of the Christian Church*, 3d ed. New York: Oxford University Press, 2005.
Davis, Cyprian. "The *Didache* and Early Monasticism in the East and West." In *The Didache in Context: Essays on Its Text, History and Transmission.* Ed. Clayton N. Jefford. Leiden: E.J. Brill, 1995: 352-67.
Draper, Jonathan A. "A Commentary on the *Didache* in Light of the Dead Sea Scrolls and related Documents." Ph. D. diss., St. John's College, Cambridge, 1983.
———. "The Jesus Tradition in the *Didache*." In *The Jesus Tradition Outside the Gospels.* Ed. D. Wenham. Sheffield: JSOT Press, 1984.
———. "Torah and Troublesome Apostles in the Didache Community." *Novum Testamentum* 33, no. 4 (1991): 347-72.
———. "Social Ambiguity and the Production of Text: Prophets, Teachers, Bishops, and Deacons and the Development of the Jesus Tradition in the Community of the *Didache*." In *The Didache in Context: Essays on Its Text, History and Transmission.* Ed. Clayton N. Jefford. Leiden: E.J. Brill, 1995: 284-312.
———. "The *Didache* in Modern Research." In *The Didache in Modern Research.* Ed. Jonathan A. Draper. Leiden: E.J. Brill, 1996: 1-42.
———. "The Jesus Tradition in the *Didache*." In *The Didache in Modern Research.* Ed. Jonathan A. Draper. Leiden: E.J. Brill, 1996: 72-91.

———. "Christian Self-definition against the 'Hypocrites' in *Didache* 8." In *The Di-dache in Modern Research*. Ed. Jonathan A. Draper. Leiden: E.J. Brill, 1996: 223-43.

———. "Torah and Troublesome Apostles in the Didache Community." In *The Didache in Modern Research*. Ed. Jonathan A. Draper. Leiden: E.J. Brill, 1996: 340-63.

———. "The Apostolic Fathers: The *Didache*." *The Expository Times* 117, no. 5 (2006): 177-181.

Dunn, James D.G. *The Partings of the Ways Between Christianity and Judaism and Their Significance for the Character of Christianity*. London: SCM Press; Philadelphia: Trinity Press International, 1991.

———. *Unity and Diversity in the New Testament*, 3rd Edition. London: SCM Press, 2006.

Ehrman, Bart. *Lost Scriptures: Books that Did Not Make It into the New Testament*. New York: Oxford University Press, 2003.

———. *Apostolic Fathers: Volume I: I Clement, II Clement, Ignatius, Polycarp, Didache*. *Loeb Classic Library 24*. Cambridge, MA: Harvard University Press, 2003.

———. *Apostolic Fathers: Volume II: Epistles of Barnabas, Papias and Quadratus, Epistle to Diognetus, The Shepherd of Hermas*. *Loeb Classic Library 25*. Cambridge, MA: Harvard University Press, 2003.

Ferguson, Everett, Michael P. McHugh, Frederick W. Norris. *Encyclopedia of Early Christianity*, 2d ed. New York: Garland Pub., 1999.

Flusser, David. "A Rabbinic Parallel to the Sermon on the Mount [and *Did. 3]*." In *Judaism and the Origins of Christianity*. Jerusalem: Magnes, 1988: 494-508.

———. "Paul's Jewish-Christian Opponents in the *Didache*." In *The Didache in Modern Research*. Ed. Jonathan A. Draper. Leiden: E.J. Brill, 1996: 195-211.

Frend, W.H.C. *The Rise of Christianity*. Philadelphia: Fortress, 1984.

Garrow, A.J.P. *The Gospel of Matthew's Dependence on the Didache*. London/New York: T&T Clark International, 2004.

Glover, R. "The *Didache's* Quotations and the Synoptic Gospels." *NTS* 5 (1958-59): 12-29.

Goodspeed, E.J. "The *Didache*, Barnabas and the Doctrina." *ATR* 27 (1945): 228-47.

Grenfell, Bernard P., and Hunt, Arthur S., eds. *Oxyrhynchus Papyri*, Part XV. London: Egypt Exploration Society, 1922: 12-15.

Grosvenor, Edwin A. "An Interview with Bishop Bryennios-The Discovery of the Teaching." *Andover Review* (Nov. 1884): 515-16.

de Halleux, Andre. "Ministers in the *Didache*." In *The Didache in Modern Research*. Ed. Jonathan A. Draper. Leiden: E.J. Brill, 1996: 300-20.

Harnack, Adolf von. *Die Lehre der Zwölf Apostel: Texte und Untersuchungen zur Geschichte der Altchristlichen Literatur*. Vol. 2. Leipzig: Hinrichs, 1886: 1-70.

———. *The Mission and Expansion of Christianity in the First Three Centuries*. 2 vols. Translated by J. Moffatt from the 1905 German original. New York: G.P. Putman's Sons, 1908.

———. "Didache" in *New Schaff-Herzog Encyclopedia of Religious Knowledge*, Volume III: 420-24.

Harris, J. Rendel. *The Teaching of the Apostles: Newly Edited, with Facsimile Text and a Commentary*. London: C.J. Clay, 1887.

Henderson, Ian H. "*Didache* and Orality in the Synoptic Comparison." *JBL* 111 (1992): 283-306.

———. "Style Switching in the *Didache*: Fingerprint or Argument." In *The Didache in Context: Essays on Its Text, History and Transmission*. Ed. Clayton N. Jefford. Leiden: E.J. Brill, 1995: 179-209.

Hengel, Martin. *The Four Gospels and the One Gospel of Jesus Christ.* Harrisburg: Trinty Press, 2000.

Hennecke, Edgar. *New Testament Apocrypha.* 2 vols. Ed. Wilhelm Schneemelcher. Translated by R. Mcl. Wilson from the 1959 German original. Philadelphia: Westminster, 1965.

Hitchcock, Roswell D., and Francis Brown, eds. *Teaching of the Twelve Apostles: Edited with Translation, Introduction and Notes.* New York: Charles Scribner's Sons, 1884.

Holmes, Michael W. *The Apostolic Fathers: Greek Texts and English Translations.* Grand Rapids: Baker Books, 1999.

Horner, G. *The Statutes of the Apostles.* London: Williams & Norgate, 1904.

———. "A New Papyrus Fragment of the *Didache* in Coptic." *JTS* 25 (1924): 225-31.

Jay, Eric G. "From Presbyter-Bishops to Bishops and Presbyters." *The Second Century* 1 (1981): 125-62.

Jefford, Clayton N. *The Sayings of Jesus in the Teaching of the Twelve Apostles.* Supplements to *Vigiliae Christianae* 11. Leiden: E.J. Brill, 1989.

———. "Presbyters in the community of the *Didache*." In *Studia Patristica* 21. Ed. Elizabeth A. Livingstone. Leuven: Peeters Press, 1989: 122-28.

———. "Did Ignatius of Antioch Know the *Didache*?" In *The Didache in Context: Essays on Its Text, History and Transmission*. Ed. Clayton N. Jefford. Leiden: E.J. Brill, 1995: 330-51.

———. With Kenneth J. Harder. "A Bibliography of Literature on the *Didache*." In *The Didache in Context: Essays on Its Text, History and Transmission*. Ed. Clayton N. Jefford. Leiden: E.J. Brill, 1995: 368-82.

———. "*Didache*." In *Eerdmans Dictionary of the Bible*. Ed. David Noel Freedman. Grand Rapids: Eerdmans, 2001: 345a-46a.

———. *The Apostolic Fathers: An Essential Guide.* Nashville: Abingdon Press, 2006.

Jeremias, Joachim. *Infant Baptism in the First Four Centuries.* London: SCM Press, 1960.

———. *The Origins of Infant Baptism.* London: SCM Press, 1963.

———. *The Eucharistic Words of Jesus.* Translated by Norman Perrin from the 1964 German original. New York: Charles Scribner's Sons, 1977.

Johnson, Sherman Elbridge. "A Subsidiary Motive for the Writing of the *Didache*." In *Munera Studiosa*. Ed. S.E. Johnson et al. Cambridge, MA: Episcopal Divinity School, 1946: 107-22.

Jones, F. Stanley, and Paul A. Mirecki. "Considerations on the Coptic Papyrus of the *Didache*." In *The Didache in Context: Essays on Its Text, History and Transmission*. Ed. Clayton N. Jefford. Leiden: E.J. Brill, 1995: 47-87.

Kleist, James A. *The Didache, The Epistle of Barnabas, et al., Newly Translated and Annotated.* Westminster, MD: Newman, 1961: 3-25.

Kloppenborg, John S. "*Didache* 16:6-8 and Special Matthaean Tradition." *Zeitschrift für die Neutestamentliche Wissenschaft* 70 (1979): 54-67.

———. "The Transformation of Moral Exhortation in *Didache* 1-5." In *The Didache in Context: Essays on Its Text, History and Transmission*. Ed. Clayton N. Jefford. Leiden: E.J. Brill, 1995: 88-109.

Koester, Helmut. *Synoptische Überlieferung bei den Apostolischen Vätern.* Texte und Untersuchungen: Berlin, 1957.

Kraft, Robert A. *Barnabas and the Didache.* New York: Thomas Nelson & Sons, 1965.

————. *The Apostolic Fathers: A New Translation and Commentary.* Toronto: Thomas Nelson, 1965: 1-16, 57-178.

————. "The Didache" in *Anchor Bible Dictionary.* Ed. David Noel Freedman. New York: Doubleday, 1990, II: 197-98.

Ladd, George Eldon. "The Eschatology of the *Didache.*" Ph.D. diss., Harvard University, 1949.

Layton, B. "The Sources, Date and Transmission of *Didache.* 1.3b-2.1." *HTR* 61 (1968): 343-83.

Lightfoot, J.B. *The Apostolic Fathers: Revised Texts with Short Introductions and English Translations.* London: Macmillan, 1912: 215-35.

Massaux, Edouard. "The Problem of the *Didache.*" In *The Influence of the Gospel of Saint Matthew on Christian Literature before Saint Irenaeus.* Macon, GA: Mercer University Press, 1993: 3:17-73.

Milavec, Aaron. "The Pastoral Genius of the *Didache.*" In *Religious Writings and Religious Systems.* Ed. Jacob Neusner et al. Brown Studies in Religion 2. Atlanta: Scholars Press, 1989: 2:89-125.

————. "Distinguishing True and False Prophet: The Protective Wisdom of the *Didache.*" *Journal of Early Christian Studies* 2, no. 2 (1994): 117-36.

————. "The Social Setting of 'Turning the Other Cheek' and 'Loving One's Enemies' in Light of the *Didache.*" *BTB* 25, no. 2 (1995): 131-43.

————. "The Economic Safety Net in the *Didache.*" *Proceedings of the Easters Great Lakes Biblical Society* 16 (1996): 73-84.

————. "How the *Didache* Attracted, Cooled Down, and Quenched Prophetic Fire." *Proceedings of the Eastern Great Lakes & Midwest Bible Society* 19 (1999): 103-17.

————. "Synoptic Tradition in the *Didache* Revisited." *Journal of Early Christian Studies* 11, no. 4 (2003): 443-80.

————. *The Didache: Faith, Hope, and Life of the Early Christian Communities, 50-70 C.E.* Mahwah, NJ: The Newman Press, 2003.

————. *The Didache: Text, Translation Analysis and Commentary.* Collegeville, MN: Liturgical Press, 2003.

Mitchell, Nathan. "Baptism in the *Didache.*" In *The Didache in Context: Essays on Its Text, History and Transmission.* Ed. Clayton N. Jefford. Leiden: E.J. Brill, 1995: 226-55.

Moule, C.F.D. "A Note on *Didache* IX. 4." *NTS* 6 (1955): 240-43.

————. "A Reconsideration of the Context of Maranatha." *NTS* 6 (1960): 307-10.

Niederwimmer, Kurt. "Der Didachist und seine Quellen." In *The Didache in Context: Essays on Its Text, History and Transmission.* Ed. Clayton N. Jefford. Leiden: E.J. Brill, 1995: 15-36.

————. "An Examination of the Development of Itinerant Radicalism in the Environment and Tradition in the *Didache.*" In *The Didache in Context: Essays on Its Text, History and Transmission.* Ed. Clayton N. Jefford. Leiden: E.J. Brill, 1995: 321-39.

————. *The Didache.* Translated by Linda M. Maloney from the 1989 German original. Minneapolis: Fortress, 1998.

Oulton, J.E.L. "Clement of Alexandria and the *Didache.*" *JTS* 41 (1940): 177-79.

Pardee, Nancy. "The Curse that Saves (*Didache* 16:5)." In *The Didache in Context: Essays on Its Text, History and Transmission.* Ed. Clayton N. Jefford. Leiden: E.J. Brill, 1995: 156-76.

————. "The Genre of the *Didache*: A Text-Linguistic Analysis," Ph.D. diss. University of Chicago, 2002.

Patterson, Stephen J. "Didache 11-13: The Legacy of Radical Itineracy in Early Christianity." In *The Didache in Context: Essays on Its Text, History and Transmission.* Ed. Clayton N. Jefford. Leiden: E.J. Brill, 1995: 313-29.

Quasten, Johannes. *Patrology.* 1950. Reprint, Utrecht: Spectrum, 1975.

Reed, Jonathan. "The Hebrew Epic and the *Didache.*" In *The Didache in Context: Essays on Its Text, History and Transmission.* Ed. Clayton N. Jefford. Leiden: E.J. Brill, 1995: 213-25.

Richardson, Cyril C., ed. and trans. *Early Christian Fathers: Newly Translated and Edited.* Philadelphia: Westminster, 1953: 167-79.

Riggs, John W. "From Gracious Table to Sacramental Elements: The Tradition-History of *Didache* 9 and 10." *The Second Century* 4, no.2 (1956): 83-101.

Roberts, Colin Henderson. *Manuscript, Society and Belief in Early Christian Egypt* (London: Oxford, 1979): 10-15.

Robinson, J. Armitage. *Barnabas, Hermas and the Didache.* London, 1920.

———. "The Epistle of Barnabas and the *Didache.*" *JTS* 35 (1934): 113-46, 225-48.

Robinson, John A.T. *Redating the New Testament.* Philadelphia: Westminster Press, 1976.

Rordorf, Willy. *Sunday: The History of the Day of Rest and Worship.* Philadelphia: Westminster, 1968.

———. "The *Didache.*" In *The Eucharist of the Early Christians.* Ed. Willy Rordorf et al. Translated by M.J. O'Connell. Collegeville, MN: Liturgical Press, 1978: 1-23.

———. "The Lord's Prayer in the Light of its Liturgical Use in the Early Church." *Studia Liturgica* 14 (1980): 1-19.

———. "Does the D*idache* Contain Jesus Tradition Independently of the Synoptic Gospels?" In *Jesus and the Oral Synoptic Tradition.* Ed. Henry Wansbrough. Sheffield: Sheffield Academic Press, 1991: 394-423. Reprinted in Rordorf 1993: 330-59.

———. *La doctrine des douze apôtres.* 1978 edition republished containing an updated bibliography, 211-20, and extended notes revising and completing an earlier edition, 221-46. Paris: Cerf, 1998.

Sabatier, Paul. *La Didachè or L'enseignement des douze apôtres.* Paris: Librairie Fischbacher, 1885.

Schaff, P. *The Oldest Church Manual Called the Teaching of the Twelve Apostles,* 2d ed. Edinburgh: Clark, 1887.

Schnelle, Udo. *The History and Theology of the New Testament Writings.* Translated by M. Eugene Boring. Minneapolis: Fortress Press, 1998.

Schöllgen, Georg. "The *Didache* as Church Order: An Examination of the Purposes for the Composition of the *Didache* and its Consequences for its Interpretation." In *The Didache in Modern Research.* ed. Jonathan Draper. Leiden: E.J. Brill, 1996: 43-71.

Seeliger, Hans Reinhard. "Considerations on the Background and Purpose of the Apocalyptic Final Chapter of the *Didache.*" In *The Didache in Modern Research.* Ed. Jonathan A. Draper. Leiden: E.J. Brill, 1996: 373-82.

Skarsaune, Oskar. *The Proof from Prophecy.* Leiden: E.J. Brill, 1987.

———. *In the Shadow of the Temple.* Downers Grove, IL: InterVarsity Press, 2002.

Skehan, Patrick William. "*Didache* 1,6 and Sirach 12,1." *Biblica* 44 (1963): 533-36.

Slee, Michelle. *The Church in Antioch in the First Century CE.* Sheffield: Sheffield Academic Press, 2003.

Smyth, Egbert. "Baptism in *Didache* and in Early Christian Art." *Andover Review* (Nov, 1884): 533-47.

Smith, M.A. "Did Justin Know the *Didache?*" *Studia Patristica* 7 (1966): 287-90.

Sparks, Jack N., ed. and trans. "The Teaching of the Twelve Apostles." In *The Apostolic Fathers*. Nashville: Thomas Nelson, 1978.

Stark, Rodney. *The Rise of Christianity: A Sociologist Reconsiders History*. Princeton: Princeton University Press, 1996.

Streeter, H. "The Much-belaboured *Didache*." *JTS* 37 (1936): 369-74.

———. "Origin and Date of the Didache," in *The Primitive Church*. New York: Macmillan Co., 1929, 286-94.

Suggs, M.J. "The Christian Two-Way Tradition." In *Studies in the New Testament and Early Christian Literature*. Leiden: E.J. Brill, 1972: 60-74.

Taylor, C. *The Teaching of the Twelve Apostles with Illustrations from the Talmud*. Cambridge: Deighton Bell, 1886.

Telfer, W. "The *Didache* and the Apostolic Synod of Antioch." *JTS* 40 (1939): 133-46, 258-71.

———. "The 'Plot' of the *Didache*." *JTS* 45 (1944): 141-51.

Tuckett, C.M. "The Sabbath, Sunday, and the Law in Luke/Acts." In *From Sabbath to Lord's Day: A Biblical, Historical, and Theological Investigation*. Ed. D.A. Carson. Grand Rapids: Zondervan, 1982.

———. "Synoptic Tradition in the *Didache*." In *The Didache in Modern Research*. Ed. Jonathan A. Draper. Leiden: E.J. Brill, 1996: 92-128.

Tuilier, Andre, "La *Didache* at le probleme synoptique," in *The Didache in Context*. Ed. Clayton Jefford. Leiden: E.J. Brill, 1995: 110-130.

———. "Les charismatiques itinerants dans la Didache et dans l'Evangile de Matthieu (with an English abstract)," in Van de Sandt, *Matthew and the Didache*. Assen: Royal van Gorcum; Minneapolis: Fortress, 2005: 157-72.

Tugwell, Simon. *The Apostolic Fathers*. Harrisburg, PA: Morehouse Publishing, 1990.

Turner, Eric G. *The Typology of the Early Codex*. Philadelphia: Univ. of Pennsylvania Press, 1977.

Van de Sandt, Huub, and David Flusser. *The Didache: Its Jewish Sources and Its Place in Early Judaism and Christianity*. Assen: Van Gorcum; Minneapolis: Fortress, 2002.

———. *Matthew and the Didache*. Assen: Royal van Gorcum; Minneapolis: Fortress, 2005.

Varner, William. "The *Didache*'s Use of the Old and New Testaments." *The Masters Seminary Journal* Volume 16, Number 1 (Spring, 2005): 127-151.

———. "What the *Teaching* Can Teach Us." *Christianity Today* Volume 50, Number 6 (2006): 30-32.

Del Verme, Marcello. *Didache and Judaism: The Jewish Roots of an Ancient Christian-Jewish Work*. Harrisburg, PA: Continuum, 2005.

Vokes, F.E. *The Riddle of the Didache: Fact or Fiction, Heresy or Catholicism?* London: SPCK, 1938.

———. "The Didache—Still Debated." *Church Quarterly* 3 (1970): 57-62.

Warfield, B.B. "Notes on the *Didache*" *Journal of the Exegetical Society* (June, 1886): 92-93

Wengst, Klaus. *Didache (Apostellehre), Barnabasbrief, Zweiter Klemensbrief, Schrift an Diognet*. Darmstadt: Wissenschaftliche Buchgesellschaft, 1984.

Wise, Michael, et al. *The Dead Sea Scrolls: A New Translation*. San Francisco: Harpers San Francisco, 1996.

Index of Authors

Only authors mentioned in the text are included in the Index. Other authors that were consulted are in the Bibliography.

About the Author

Dr. William Varner holds degrees from Bob Jones University, Biblical Theological Seminary, Dropsie College, and Temple University. He serves as Professor of Biblical Studies at The Masters College in Santa Clarita, CA. He came to The Master's College after seven years of pastoral ministry and seventeen years as Dean of the Institute of Biblical Studies in New Jersey. In addition to teaching Biblical Exposition and Greek courses, Dr. Varner also serves as Director of the college's IBEX semester in Israel program. He is a member of the Evangelical Theological Society and Society of Biblical Literature, has authored five other books, and has published over one hundred journal and periodical articles. He loves traveling with his wife, Helen, and has led forty one study trips to Israel. Dr. Varner was honored as The Master's College "Teacher of the Year" in 1999 and 2005 and nominated to "Who's Who among America's Teachers" from 1998-2006. Dr. Varner's interests also include military history, especially that of the Civil War.